Practical Strengths:

A CliftonStrengths® Guide to Everyday Ways

Career Success

By Jo Self

Practical Strengths

A CliftonStrengths® Guide to Everyday Ways

Career Success

By Jo Self

2022

Content Editor, Creative Partner,
and Foreword by
Jennifer Doyle Vancil, M.Ed.

For my son, O
who continually inspires me to build a
Strengths-Based Generation

I also hold the deepest gratitude for:

Jennifer
Friend, fellow coach, confidant and content editor.

Stacy Ballinger-Moles, Ed.D.
Who graciously shared her original document which
inspired this book

Samir
For introducing me to the world of strengths

Thomas
For your continuous mentoring, knowledge and insights

And finally, *Dr. Donald Clifton*, thank you for your vision
and belief in seeing what is right in people

And to *everyone* who shared their stories
and gave this book their personal touch!

Contents

For additional resources, please check out:

http://discoverjoself.com/resources

Foreword

I first met Jo Self the way many of us did, through her posts in social media on the topic of "Speaking of Strengths". And maybe like you, I was drawn to her authenticity and thoughtful conversation around the idea that we can use our strengths in every aspect of our lives.

I hired Jo to work with me when I was creating my web site because I knew she had the unique ability to take the words people say and give them back in writing with a clear strengths-based story. She calls it a "Talent Detangler", but it looks like magic to me. She helped me understand that I see career as a journey and because of her talents, the words on my web site describe clearly what I do. She used her Communication talent to put my thoughts into words, something I can do for others, but could not do for myself.

When Jo was writing her first book in the Practical Strengths series, *"Practical Strengths: Parenting"* I had the honor of writing the testimonial about being a Relator Parent and I saw in that book the incredible power of describing each of the 34 strengths and how they can be used in practical, everyday situations. The testimonials given for each of the strengths lends a voice, describing what it's like to live from that strength. It helps readers to understand personally what using that strength in practical, everyday ways can look like.

As we talked about my work as a strengths-based career coach and what was to be her next book (this one) our partnership emerged. She asked me to partner with her as a Subject-Matter Expert and serve as her editor. Leveraging our shared Communication talent by collaborating on how to put our collective thousands of hours of coaching and strengths training experience into words has been one of the most meaningful experiences of my life.

With this book, we hope to inspire you to understand that considering your unique natural talents in your career transitions and job searches is the key to finding work that you like - and will be good at. We wrote this with both jobseekers and those who help them in mind. We hope it serves as a reference for you as you seek to understand how your top strengths, or the strengths of those you are supporting, identified through the CliftonStrengths® assessment, can be used in the four following areas:

What to Look For: Gallup®'s research shows that using your strengths at work results in six times greater job satisfaction. It's our goal to help you look for jobs that use your strengths. It sounds simple, but so many of the jobseekers I've worked with have found themselves in jobs that don't use their strengths and come to me in the midst of burnout. Amazingly, though, moving to a role or setting in which they can use their top strengths changes the whole situation. The *"What to Look For"* section will guide jobseekers or those in career exploration to consider what kinds of roles or environments will feed their strengths before they start applying.

How to Look: In all my years of career coaching, I've heard the same advice given to jobseekers. "You have to network." And "Do your research." But if you know anything about strengths, you know that people with different natural talents operate differently in the world. This section helps you understand how to use your unique strengths to job search or explore careers in a way that fits YOU. A jobseeker with high Input and/or Learner will want to start with research before trying to connect with people. A jobseeker with high Communication and/or WOO may love leveraging social media to network. While someone high in Achiever will prefer a step-by-step plan and someone with Strategic will want to know any plan laid out is flexible. The *"How to Look"* section will give you some clues on how each strength can help you look for work in a way that feels most natural.

What to Communicate: Helping people communicate their strengths is my passion and Jo and I had so much fun collaborating on this part. Think of this as what you want to say in your introductions to potential hiring managers, what kind of stories to tell in your interviews, and what kind of information to include in your resumes, cover letters, and social media profiles. If you can effectively communicate what your strengths are to those who will hire you, then you'll be hired FOR your strengths instead of in spite of them. That, after all, is the goal. If you want a job where you get to use your strengths every day, you have to effectively communicate what they are. The *"What to Communicate"* section gives you some ideas on exactly that.

How to Succeed: In this section, we provide advice on how to succeed once you get your new job. The idea of this section is that each person will integrate into a new setting differently depending on their own natural talents. Those with high Relator will want to develop strong one on one relationships with their new coworkers. Those with high Responsibility will be eager to understand what they can take on and learn the boundaries of what they have authority over. Those with high Context will be interested to understand the history of the organization and how they got to where they are as that history will inform current and future decisions. Think of "How to Succeed on the Job" as your advice for your first 30 days in your new strengths-based career.

We hope this book serves as a guide to help you and those you are encouraging to create strengths-based careers. Jo and I are cheering for you!

 Jennifer Doyle Vancil, M.Ed.
Gallup® Certified Strengths Coach
Strengths-Based Career Coach and
Trainer, Communicating Strengths LLC
www.communicatingstrengths.com

The only way to do great work is to love what you do. If you haven't found it yet, keep looking. Don't settle.

Steve Jobs

Talents are naturally recurring patterns of thought, feeling, or behavior that can be productively applied

A strength is the ability to consistently provide near-perfect performance in a specific activity.

Talents, knowledge, and skills - along with the time spent practicing, developing your skills, and building your knowledge base - combine to create your strengths.

- Gallup®

Introduction

I fell in love with CliftonStrengths® way back in 2003. I was introduced to it when it was still known as StrengthsFinder by a dear friend, Samir Gupte. The moment I learned my top five talents, I was hooked. It was as if I had received a user's manual for myself! The words that had always failed me when trying to describe why I did what I did, or why I enjoyed something so much, were now laid out before me. It was life changing.

Over the years, whenever someone came to me for advice, the first thing I would ask was, "do you know your strengths?" I would immediately have them read, *Now, Discover Your Strengths*, and then have them come back to me. Knowing their top five allowed me to have a deeper understanding of who they were and who they had the potential to be. Eventually this passion led me to become one of the first Spanish-speaking Gallup® Certified Strengths coaches in 2015. It is not just a job - it's a calling.

When people ask me, "Why Strengths?" My answer is fairly simple. I believe that strengths are the short-cut glossary into the human psyche that allows us to build better relationships through better communication and greater compassion. At the end of the day, it's *why* we are and *why* we're here. I truly believe if we can just appreciate the depth of understanding these 34 talents can give us, we can improve our relationships immensely - from the most intimate to the community-at-large. Once you see yourself objectively, you have no choice but to do the same for others as well. It allows us grace with ourselves, and others, that we may not have otherwise.

While there are some amazing materials out there to help us understand our talents at a deeper level, I always felt there was a small piece missing. Much of what exists is helpful in the professional realm, but there was a void in the day-to-day use of our talents - and our talents are *always* with us. They may show up differently in our different roles (parent, sibling, employee, volunteer, etc), but they are a deeply ingrained part of us. This is what led me to decide to write this series.

By recognizing these 34 talents, and how they show up for you, you will build confidence naturally. For me, a lack of confidence is merely a symptom of a lack of self-awareness. I want you to see yourself in a positive light and understand just how much your talents guide and lead you through your daily life - from relationships to how you spend your free time and everything in between.

My hope is that this book sheds light on something you may have taken for granted. That you now see your talent as something special, something to be valued and something unique to *you*. Also, how you can now harness this talent to build a strength and how to recognize when it might be getting in the way.

In strength and love

Quick Reference: Career Success

You can find shareable graphics for each of these talents on http://discoverjoself.com/resources

ACHIEVER®: You thrive in roles where you can actively contribute to what needs to get done. Seeing the end results of your hard work is satisfying and inspires you to keep going and stay driven to the finish line.

ACTIVATOR®: You thrive in project-oriented environments, ones that have a beginning, middle and end. You especially love being involved in the start of new projects, as both the element of innovation and the chance to motivate the team excites you.

ADAPTABILITY®: You thrive in environments which allow you to pivot and change direction when the task at hand calls for it. You find energy in an environment which innovates and adapts as needs and outcomes shift.

ANALYTICAL®: You thrive in roles which require precision, facts and collecting data. You are energized by being able to fully research and investigate in areas that will affect the overall outcome, knowing that your information is a key factor.

ARRANGER®: You thrive in roles which allow you to tap into your organization genius. Whether it be forming the perfect teams, events, or projects, you shine most when flexing your coordinating muscle.

BELIEF®: You thrive in roles and organizations which are in full alignment with your own values. You are motivated to work harder for issues you believe in and companies which support your own ideologies.

COMMAND®: You thrive in organizations where there is quick opportunity for leadership. You are able to come in and take charge, lending a sense of calm to even turbulent situations.

COMMUNICATION®: You thrive in roles where there is ample opportunity to connect and speak with others - either verbally or through the written word. You create alliances and connections through your verbal prowess.

COMPETITION®: You thrive in roles where "winning" is a key motivator. Whether in teams or on your own, having your performance measured for excellence energizes you and keeps your eyes on the prize.

CONNECTEDNESS®: You thrive in environments where there is opportunity to be in community. This kind of work is both meaningful and satisfying for your soul. It's easy for you to stay motivated when your job is connected to a larger mission that you believe in.

CONSISTENCY®: You thrive in areas where clear expectations and set ground rules are required for everyone. Stability and calm are key for you in maximizing your productivity.

CONTEXT®: You thrive in roles where you can be the investigator. You enjoy researching the history of projects and opportunities which will propel projects - and people - forward by learning from the past.

DELIBERATIVE®: You thrive in roles where you can pair your cautious approach with careful decision-making and show those around you how to evaluate risks thoroughly. Your thoughtful actions translate into a sense of stability and protection.

DEVELOPER®: You thrive in roles where you have the chance to encourage and cultivate the special abilities of those around you. You are able to celebrate each unique step in the journey of others, recognizing that every step is a step forward.

DISCIPLINE®: You thrive in environments where structure and routine are the order of the day. You are motivated to keep track of the details and schedules ensuring that everyone stays on task.

EMPATHY®: You thrive in roles which allow you to give input on the overall culture, the emotional wellbeing of team members, and have a service-oriented mission. you have an incredible capacity to hold space for others.

FOCUS®: You thrive in environments where there are clear cut objectives and you are able to keep your eye on the target, prioritize your tasks, hit the deadlines, and accomplish the goals.

FUTURISTIC®: You thrive in environments which allow you to dream, share your visions, and work toward a common goal. You are energized by "tomorrow" and "what if" scenarios which allow your imagination to explore all the possibilities.

HARMONY®: You thrive in environments where there is a high collaborative focus and low competition among co-workers. You are also a natural mediator and serve well in situations where an objective third party is required.

IDEATION®: You thrive in environments that provide the freedom to express your ideas and creativity. Brainstorming is your superpower and requires a space where it is valued and appreciated.

INCLUDER®: You thrive in environments which allow you to be part of a group or team. Being a team leader is something you may enjoy since you easily create a feeling of togetherness.

INDIVIDUALIZATION®: You thrive in roles which give you the opportunity to make a personal impact and give recognition to others. You excel when you can help others realize and act upon their potential.

INPUT®: You thrive in environments which will allow you to research innovative ideas or find new ways of doing things and then sharing what you know with others. You are a master resourcer.

INTELLECTION®: You thrive in environments which allow for in-depth discussion with colleagues and where sharing ideas is encouraged. Asking deep questions and having time to think things through is a "must have" for you.

LEARNER®: You thrive in environments where you can continuously be exposed to new information and experiences and can share what you learn with others. You value environments that prioritize training and development.

MAXIMIZER®: You thrive in environments which allow you to set the pace, build on existing processes or programs to improve them, or to develop the strengths of others so they may serve in their own excellence.

POSITIVITY®: You thrive in organizations which see solutions over problems, promote a convivial and friendly culture, and allow you to be the cheerleader for those around you. You are a natural promoter.

RELATOR®: You thrive in opportunities which allow you to foster long-term relationships, have one-on-ones on a regular basis, and work closely with a tight knit team. You prioritize people over tasks.

RESPONSIBILITY®: You thrive in positions which have clear job duties and expectations are well defined. You appreciate that both outcome and process are celebrated and recognized.

RESTORATIVE™: You thrive in environments which allow you to solve challenging problems. You don't fear a challenge, but rather enjoy identifying issues and navigating complex and difficult situations.

SELF-ASSURANCE®: You thrive in environments which allow you to have a certain amount of autonomy in your decision making, where you are surrounded by a competent team and there is a clear path for leadership roles.

SIGNIFICANCE®: You thrive in organizations where making a big impression and having a lasting impact are part of the core vision and purpose. You easily step into the spotlight.

STRATEGIC®: You thrive in roles where creativity and flexibility are part of your everyday responsibilities and there's more than one way to reach a goal. You love exploring multiple paths to a destination.

WOO®: You thrive in roles where networking and speaking with others is a key part of your position as people naturally gravitate to you. You prefer social interaction over solitary roles.

Start where you are.

Use what you have.

Do what you can.

Arthur Ashe

WHAT would
HAPPEN if **we**
studied what was
right with people
VERSUS what's
wrong with people?

Don Clifton

Photo courtesy of Gallup, Inc. Used with permission.

HOW TO USE THIS BOOK

Obviously, your first thought is to read about your own talents. However, I hope you will share this book with others and use it to try and understand them a bit better as well.

Quick Reference (The "Twitter" statement)

This is a brief description to sum up the beauty of your talent. You can even find a meme for each one to share here: http://discoverjoself.com/resources

The Gallup® Definition

This is how Gallup® defines the talent at its best and what anyone with this talent will recognize.

Celebrate & Evaluate

Here you'll find four bullet points under each heading. *Celebrate*: I want you to see the amazing value your talent brings to the table. These are ways in which you shine. *Evaluate*: You'll find questions to ask yourself to help you harness your talent and be aware of when it might be hindering you instead of helping you.

The Description

Four main categories are considered: *What to look for, How to search, What to communicate,* and *How to succeed* to explore how each talent shines as it pertains to the job search and career success. It also sheds a small light on how it may hinder you, so you can begin to think about these aspects as well.

Coaching Questions

Four questions for you to consider a bit more deeply. Use the space in the book, or in your own journal, to reflect on these questions and try to recognize your talent in your own life.

Have fun. Explore. Talk about it with your friends and family. And, most of all, discover the power within YOU.

Being an Achiever makes me want to finish things. I get a sense of accomplishment when I finish a task no matter how big or small. Even when I start a puzzle of 1000 pieces I want to keep going until it's done.

It can be a downfall because I can rush trying to get something accomplished and sometimes I drain myself. Other times it can be really helpful because it helps me stay motivated. In school I work hard to achieve good grades because it makes me feel accomplished. There's something about finishing a project and knowing you did a good job that's really satisfying. In sports it's about constantly striving to learn a new skill and get better and celebrating each accomplishment.

I'm driven to do hard things like taking challenging classes, getting accepted into a competitive admission college and challenging myself to pursue a career in space science. And I like to be busy at work. I recently left a restaurant job that had too much down time and moved to a setting that stays constantly busy. Whatever I do, I want to reach 100% success. I've had to learn to accept I can't be perfect, but I always strive to be. Being an Achiever motivates me to keep working hard to accomplish hard things, regardless of the outcome.

Achiever®

ACHIEVER® for Career Success

You thrive in roles where you can actively contribute to what needs to get done. Seeing the end results of your hard work is satisfying and inspires you to keep going and stay driven to the finish line.

According to Gallup®: People exceptionally talented in the Achiever theme work hard and possess a great deal of stamina. They take immense satisfaction in being busy and productive.

Celebrate:

- How goals drive you
- Your to-do lists
- Your ability to work hard
- How you get things done

Evaluate:

- Am I becoming a workaholic?
- Am I expecting the same intensity from others?
- Am I forgetting about self-care?
- Am I adding too many things to my list?

What to look for: It's important for you to seek positions where there are opportunities to excel, tasks that challenge you, and places where you have control over workflow and productivity. Being task or project driven will fuel your need for a sense of accomplishment.

How to search: You are diligent, and this enables productive job searches. Break down the search into small steps and make a list of tasks. Make a list of companies you want to research, jobs you plan to apply to, and people who would be valuable to connect with, and then one by one, complete those steps. Arrange certain hours per day to focus on the job search and take breaks so as not to burnout in the process.

What to communicate: You bring a high work ethic, productivity, energy, and desire to accomplish things. Before the interview, create a list of talking points to help you prepare. Give examples of your achievements in past roles that had positive, measurable results. Share awards or accomplishments you've been recognized for or are proud of.

How to succeed: You will likely come out of the gate strong, setting the performance bar high; remember to pace yourself to prevent burnout in your new position. Be sure to keep your checklist in check and that you don't - nor allow others to - put too much on your plate. Manage your time spent on tasks, allowing time to build relationships with your new colleagues.

Sharpen your talent with these questions:

What types of tasks do you most enjoy doing and where will you have the opportunity to do them regularly?

What are the action steps you need to take to get the job you want?

What are your past key accomplishments and how can you relate them to the new position?

How can you effectively manage how much work you have on your plate?

Kristin W-S, USA

Activator makes me highly motivated & quick to act in finding the best solution or attaining a goal. Recently I learned a new technology. Within 24 hours I had set up a consultation call, created a sample application, and started implementing.

Early in life I didn't recognize these traits as strengths. People assumed I was overly confident, thought I was better and didn't want or need other people. That was completely not true and it took me years to understand and embrace that these traits ARE strengths.

Looking back over my career choices I see how Activator helped me immensely. I started a non-profit with no prior knowledge because managing complex situations & innovation come natural to me. I didn't think about failing, I was focused on the goal. Motivating and encouraging others are also big traits for me. I've owned salons for 20 years now and much of why I continue is the joy I experience when stylists achieve their own goals.

Understanding my Activator allows me to see myself as much more than just a "get it done" person. I recognize that when I focus on goals that have a positive impact on society, I am my best self and am able to bring that out in others. That is my career sweet spot.

Activator®

ACTIVATOR® for Career Success

> *You thrive in project-oriented environments, ones that have a beginning, middle and end. You especially love being involved in the start of new projects, as both the element of innovation and the chance to motivate the team excites you.*

According to Gallup®: People exceptionally talented in the Activator theme can make things happen by turning thoughts into action. They want to do things now, rather than simply talk about them.

Celebrate:

- Jumping in with no fear
- Your hands-on learning approach.
- Your ability to innovate.
- Asking "why not?" instead of "why?"

Evaluate:

- Am I rushing my decision?
- Do I act impulsively?
- Am I communicating my ideas clearly?
- Is my impatience warranted?

What to look for: It's important for you to seek positions where you take on either leadership roles or have an opportunity to move up, as well as careers that involve short-term projects to initiate. Roles where you have the autonomy to act independently or ask others to take action will suit you best.

How to search: You are motivated to jump in and start early, making quick progress on the job search so be sure to have a strategy so that your actions are getting you closer to your goal. You may need to temper the inaction of employers and length of response time and use the time for thank you emails and following up. Find support and accountability to ensure you follow through on your initial actions.

What to communicate: You bring initiative and motivation when starting new projects or meeting new people. You easily give quick and decisive answers, due to your previous preparation, which comes across as confident and capable. You are good at translating thoughts into persuasive action. When you interview, give examples of how actions you've initiated contributed to positive outcomes or results.

How to succeed: You make a great first impression with new employers as you quickly demonstrate how you complete complex tasks efficiently. Remember to share the work and compromise with your new team to accomplish tasks.

Sharpen your talent with these questions:

Which roles allow for more project style work in which action can be taken regularly?

How can you follow-up proactively while waiting for a response to your application or interview?

When have you managed complex projects in the past or motivated others to work together?

Who can help you understand what actions you have the autonomy to initiate?

Stacy B, USA

Automotive, Retail, Energy, Technology, Veterinarian....

These are some of the industries I've worked in, across numerous companies, the past 25 years. Adaptability is the key strength that has allowed me to shift industries and companies. Yet, while it can be a tremendous asset, it can also have its disadvantages if not managed correctly. At my best, I thrive working in environments that are constantly changing with tight deadlines. Rather than being frazzled with so much to do in a short amount of time, it calms and focuses me, allowing me to quickly prioritize what needs to be done and helping others stay calm amidst shifting priorities. "Keep calm and carry on" is a mantra that seems written just for me. There are downsides to having high Adaptability. One is taking on too much and being reactive versus proactive and appearing that you have accomplished little, in addition to being taken advantage of and for granted. It can also be a detriment in environments that value stability and routine, or where detailed planning is required. The key if you have high Adaptability is to seek out organizations where the ability to manage change is valued. Also, leveraging other strengths and partnering with those with strengths that are complementary.

Adaptability®

ADAPTABILITY® for Career Success

You thrive in environments which allow you to pivot and change direction when the task at hand calls for it. You find energy in an environment which innovates and adapts as needs and outcomes shift.

According to Gallup®: People exceptionally talented in the Adaptability theme prefer to go with the flow. They tend to be "now" people who take things as they come and discover the future one day at a time.

Celebrate:

- How you 'go with the flow'
- Your spontaneous nature
- How you adjust seamlessly to new situations
- Your flexibility

Evaluate:

- Is this change necessary?
- Am I blindly following others?
- Is my flexibility preventing clarity or understanding?
- Does this situation require a solid decision?

What to look for: You most appreciate being in flexible environments where you have some agility with your schedule, projects or responsibilities. Consider a start-up environment where things move at a faster pace and change is par for the course. You enjoy environments that require responding rather than planning.

How to search: Because you are generally able to go with the flow, be sure to establish some priorities for the job search to keep you on track and the goal in mind. Make a list of key tasks or needs you will want in your ideal job. As long as you have these key elements in mind, you might even find an opportunity where you least expect it – and that would be OK with you. You'll enjoy getting referrals to opportunities and people you didn't seek out.

What to communicate: Draw on the variety of your experiences to demonstrate your ability to be flexible and adapt. Impress them with questions that put a little more pressure on since you are quick on your feet and enjoy a chance to show off your agile mindset. While you might focus more on the here and now, be sure to express your desires for your future goals or development.

How to succeed: Be proactive where it counts. Your easy-going nature might be misinterpreted for being passive or uninterested. Volunteer for projects and find ways to show off being a "jack-of-all-trades". Put yourself into situations where responding to changing circumstances well will make you shine.

Sharpen your talent with these questions:

Is this an environment that will allow you to be at your best reacting in a changing environment?

Who else can you talk with and how can you follow advice, even unexpected, from those you're meeting as you search for a job?

When has being flexible served your past company really well and contributed to strong outcomes?

How can you show your commitment to the team by jumping in without needing a lot of preparation when others might be hesitant?

Michael R, USA

Being Analytical not only strengthens my day-to-day work as a professional, but also allowed me to switch careers and start my own company. With the desire to move from an HR Compensation specific role to a more HRIS and Data Analysis role, I was able to use my strength to highlight projects that were applicable to the job I wanted, not the job I had. It also allowed me to start my own data analysis consulting service for startups & small businesses. Not only did it help me research & start a business from scratch, but I also get to analyze data for small businesses and help them understand and make sense of their information.

I've always been a thinker, but one of the challenges was learning not to be too analytical. There's a time to analyze and there's a time to get things done. I don't always have the time I might want. In these instances, I always come back to the situation after the task is completed to analyze how I can better prepare myself for similar experiences in the future. This approach has helped me not let my Analytical get in the way of my work but allows me to make better use of it.

Analytical®

ANALYTICAL® for Career Success

You thrive in roles which require precision, facts and collecting data. You are energized by being able to fully research and investigate in areas that will affect the overall outcome, knowing that your information is a key factor.

According to Gallup®: People exceptionally talented in the Analytical theme search for reasons and causes. They have the ability to think about all of the factors that might affect a situation.

Celebrate:

- Your desire for the truth
- Your ability to ask the 'right' questions
- Your methodical decision-making process
- Your cool head in tough situations

Evaluate:

- Am I stuck in analysis paralysis?
- Am I more worried about being right than finding compromise?
- Am I considering the emotional impact – on myself and others?
- Are all these questions necessary?

What to look for: It's important for you to seek positions which require research, analysis, and data collection. You will excel in a career that emphasizes investigation and facts as a core part of the job. You'll need an environment where you can ask questions and seek out causes and effects of decisions.

How to search: You carefully review job descriptions and investigate the position before applying to make sure it is a rational choice worth pursuing. You are good at thinking realistically about the job by asking yourself strategic questions. You'll prefer to have options and weigh out the pros and cons of each, comparing companies and positions by some objective criteria.

What to communicate: You should highlight your ability to see the big picture and how all other factors may affect it. You are good at providing evidence of success through concrete examples and results. You think through all questions and present a clear solution. Give examples of when your analysis has made a measurable impact on an organization you've been part of. While you tend to stick with facts, remember to demonstrate your personality as well.

How to succeed: Offer to use your talents to help others with a final edit before a big project is submitted or to be a sounding board before decisions are put into action. Remember to think through the best way to deliver messages to your new team. Be engaging as well as detailed, also ensuring to point out the positive as well as the details of concern.

Sharpen your talent with these questions:

What types of projects or topics are you most interested in researching?

How can you best analyze the role requirements and weigh them against your own interests?

How has your research or investigative ability contributed positively in the past?

As you interact with coworkers, how can you remember to balance your need for detail with how you build relationships?

"The Juggler" is one of the synonyms for Arranger. I believe that is one reason I've thrived as a training department of one for over 25 years.

Arranger helps me with everything from course creation to delivery. As an internal trainer I know most participants and their needs which allows me to rearrange "the plan" as they show up and things change. I feel confident I can give them what they need to be successful at that moment.

My Arranger made me feel the proudest when we brought in an external trainer for our IT leadership. The trainer asked to assign people to different tables who don't normally work together. Not an easy task; but Arranger took over and I created what I thought was a good plan. The joy and pride came hearing comments like, "Wow I've not worked with 'Bob' much and I really like him!" or "'Susie' has some really great ideas, I'm glad she was at my table!!" Pure GOLD!

Of course, being a juggler means knowing exactly how many balls I can keep in the air and for how long. Otherwise, it's a mess.

Arranger®

ARRANGER® for Career Success

You thrive in roles which allow you to tap into your organization genius. Whether it be forming the perfect teams, events, or projects, you shine most when flexing your coordinating muscle.

According to Gallup®: People exceptionally talented in the Arranger theme can organize, but they also have a flexibility that complements this ability. They like to determine how all of the pieces and resources can be arranged for maximum productivity.

Celebrate:

- Your ability to multitask
- The drive to focus on multiple projects
- Your ability to simplify complex arrangements
- Your flexibility

Evaluate:

- Am I overscheduling myself or others?
- Do I lose focus by juggling too many balls at once?
- Do things fall through the cracks?
- Am I too controlling of others' schedules or routines?

What to look for: You enjoy roles and organizations with a schedule that is not routine and leans toward constant motion, tapping into your love of multitasking and where you are able to anticipate the tasks and tools needed to streamline for efficiency. You'll enjoy a job in which a changing environment requires rearranging priorities regularly.

How to search: Create a system (post-its, software, etc) to help you keep contacts, jobs and opportunities top of mind allowing you to stay organized in your search. Schedule meetings with people and find ways to fit events and new contacts in your agenda. You'll even enjoy last minute opportunities, even if it means changing your plans to take advantage of them.

What to communicate: Demonstrate where your ability to multitask in other roles has helped you be both flexible and efficient as well as leading to a successful outcome. Talk about your agility to manage projects, handle last-minute requests, and delegate to the right people; this shows you have the skills necessary for faster paced environments and that you can work well under pressure.

How to succeed: Use your organizational skills to create a social meeting with each of your colleagues to get to know them better. Show off your ability to jump in and tackle the tasks at hand by being proactive with current projects.

Sharpen your talent with these questions:

What kind of roles will allow you to be the most flexible and agile?

What should you prioritize in the first 30, 60, 90 days and how will your long-term priorities differ from what's required in the short term?

How can you convey the ideas and reasoning behind your organizational structures?

How can you match people and resources to make efficient teams for the project?

Patrice P, USA

My work centers on diversity, equity, and inclusion. I liken my Belief to what some may call faith, *"Now faith is the substance of things hoped for, the evidence of things not seen."* This belief drives my work.

Belief is a feeling that I can't explain but I KNOW to be true. It usually has no proof; I am its proof. My actions make my Belief fact and takes it from being a wish to being something intangible that others also follow. My passion is to truly make dreams come true. If we were to dream of a world that is IDEAL (inclusive, diverse, equitable, accessible, and loving) supporting that belief with action we can change the world!

Belief drives me to actively choose trust. I've learned to trust myself to know that I can assist in the journey of DEI without excluding someone who may not be as far along as I 'think' they should be. And I've learned to trust others. Overwhelmingly I found people have the capacity and desire to change but lack the confidence and understanding on how to do it and feel courageous in that transformation.

Belief®

BELIEF® for Career Success

You thrive in roles and organizations which are in full alignment with your own values. You are motivated to work harder for issues you believe in and companies which support your own ideologies.

According to Gallup®: People exceptionally talented in the Belief theme have certain core values that are unchanging. Out of these values emerges a defined purpose for their lives.

Celebrate:

- Your deeply developed values
- Your sense of meaning and purpose
- Your altruistic nature
- Your strong sense of integrity

Evaluate:

- Am I too set in my ways?
- Am I open to others belief systems?
- Are my opinions too strong or too rigid?
- Am I not allowing for "grey areas"?

What to look for: It is important for you to find opportunities where you feel fully aligned with the vision and mission of the company. You should also evaluate the level of commitment the organization will have to your development as you are someone who commits fully when you believe in the cause.

How to search: Research the background and history of the companies which interest you to see if they are the kind of organization that "walks the talk". Make a list of opportunities that align with your core values. Knowing where you "draw the line" will help you evaluate the match between you and the job you choose.

What to communicate: Talk about how your sense of purpose supports your level of commitment to both a team and the organization. You may speak passionately, conveying just how motivated you are to contribute to the success of your team and the company overall. Be sure to keep an open mind and listen carefully as well to avoid sounding judgmental or rigid.

How to succeed: Let your commitment shine by being a supportive team player early on. Be sure to maintain balance in sharing opinions or reactions as you get to know your new colleagues, avoiding touchy subjects until a deeper level of trust is built.

Sharpen your talent with these questions:

What are the issues or values which most motivate you?

Which company's goals line up with matters you're passionate about?

How does this job line up with what you find meaningful and how does that drive you to accomplish tasks?

How can you be comfortable in a "gray zone" with colleagues whose beliefs may differ from yours?

Eduardo V., USA

Although I haven't consciously invested time to develop my Command talent, I've come to realize it's been a behind-the-scenes motivator in my life. When I am leading a training or facilitating a workshop in front of a group of strangers, I can often hear the unspoken elephant in the room and I'm willing to speak up about it even if I believe it's risky. When I'm on a team and there's a hesitation about next steps, my Command compels me to speak up and push the group to get started. At work, colleagues often come to me to ask for my opinion about a decision that they're wrestling with. Even when I don't trust myself, I have been surprised how often people follow my lead in a situation or business venture.

I have had conflicts with managers when I feel a lack of clarity around expectations. And I am easily annoyed when I feel stunted or blocked around expressing my opinions or suggestions. Perhaps, my presence is threatening to a manager, and I may come across to someone as not easily coachable or "manageable".

Command®

COMMAND® for Career Success

You thrive in organizations where there is quick opportunity for leadership. You are able to come in and take charge, lending a sense of calm to even turbulent situations.

According to Gallup®: People exceptionally talented in the Command theme have presence. They can take control of a situation and make decisions.

Celebrate:

- Your ability to take charge when needed
- How you keep cool in a crisis
- Your honest and candid nature
- Your willingness to confront tough situations

Evaluate:

- Am I being perceived as argumentative or forceful by others?
- Am I asking or am I telling?
- Do I take over even when not asked or I don't need to?
- Am I coming across as intimidating to others?

What to look for: It's important for you to find opportunities where there are immediate leadership responsibilities or there is a clear development path to leading. Someone with Command is likely to thrive in an organization that is experiencing change where they can lead. Perhaps, a company in the middle of restructuring would welcome your assertive approach. What feels like chaos to others feels like a welcome challenge to you.

How to search: You have a clear idea of what you are looking for in a job and a company. Combine this with your network and the expertise of others, remaining open to their suggestions, and you will have a head start as you start your search. Look for organizations which welcome challenging the status quo. Ask questions about the culture of the companies you are researching.

What to communicate: Share past decisions to difficult situations where you used your calm assertiveness in the face of challenges. Ask about leadership opportunities if they aren't immediately clear. Let them know that when you challenge an idea, it's not about conflict, but about gaining a deeper understanding and making the best decisions.

How to succeed: Get to know your team and their strengths, this will help you know how to be the leader for them. Remember to ask questions and solicit feedback. While you are comfortable with being challenged, not everyone will be as at ease as you. You might seek out a mentor who can help you develop your path to excellence.

Sharpen your talent with these questions:

What project, group or organization is facing crises or changes and could use your leadership?

Where will your assertiveness be most appreciated?

When have you made a difficult decision and how can you share the results of that in an interview?

Are you taking any unnecessary risks that could harm the people that follow you?

Jo S, USA

Communication has served me well over the years. From being a server who described the mouthwatering daily special - and as a result had the highest sales - to being the company liaison, helping employees understand what was really meant by the corporate newsletters. Nothing bothers me more than mass communications which offer more questions than answers.

It's even why I'm writing this book; my mission is to teach CliftonStrengths® as a second language. I believe in the power of words to transform.

However, I can also get so excited that I finish your sentences for you or forget to listen fully to what you have to say. My tactic to combat this bad habit? I physically put my finger over my mouth to remind me to use my two ears as much as my one mouth.

I also recognize it is a superpower of mine. It's what led to creating my famous "Talent Detangler". I always thought of it as taking dictation, but after hearing several people say, "How do you do *that*?!" I realized it might just be something special – something not everyone can do – who knew?

Communication®

COMMUNICATION® for Career Success

> *You thrive in roles where there is ample opportunity to connect and speak with others - either verbally or through the written word. You create alliances and connections through your verbal prowess.*

According to Gallup®: People exceptionally talented in the Communication theme generally find it easy to put their thoughts into words. They are good conversationalists and presenters.

Celebrate:

- Your ability to tell a captivating story
- Your clear explanations
- Being a good sounding board for others
- Your verbal processing skills

Evaluate:

- Am I listening as much as I'm talking?
- Am I missing what others are saying because I'm planning what to say next?
- Am I being clear and concise?
- Am I repeating myself too much?

What to look for: It is important to find roles where you can develop in areas such as public speaking, customer service or written communication and put your abilities to use regularly. You will shine in any role where your gift of words serves as a bridge or connection to others.

How to search: Since you articulate yourself well, expressing both what you are looking for and the value you bring in cover letters and interviews comes easily. Tap into your broad network and communicate to them what your goals are. Consider sharing your accomplishments and ideas in social media so others understand what you do well.

What to communicate: Use your storytelling ability to vividly share your past successes and experiences, connecting emotionally to your interviewer through your words and imagery. You'll form a warm connection easily with others and this will demonstrate both confidence and your ability to build trust.

How to succeed: Since you connect easily, making new friends on the job should be easy. Listen to their stories and get to know your colleagues, using your own stories as a link for connection.

Sharpen your talent with these questions:

What is your favorite way of communicating and which roles fit that style?

Who can you meet with to discuss opportunities or seek advice or introductions from?

What are one or two stories that clearly demonstrate the value you will bring to the job?

How can you identify the key players with whom you need to keep an open dialogue?

Abdulsatter A, Saudi Arabia

What motivates me every single day is the drive of competition; I just love to be number one. When I was starting out, my boss told me 'You are so competitive you want to attend every single meeting, you're still a junior you can't attend Business Leadership Meetings, it's only for seniors. My response? "Then how will I learn and grow?" The competition in me was speaking out loud!

At a recent training I did a poor job in my ICF Transcendence Coaching where I was asked to coach in front of 20 participants. It affected me deeply – to the point of tears - as I looked bad in front of myself and in front of my peers. But the competition in me helps me to recognize that I must show others how well I can do what I do. I spent weeks coaching every single person I know until I cracked it.

I've learned that overdoing it has a negative impact. I can motivate others and others know I won't accept NO as an answer. But I must be careful not to push too hard or set the bar too high as this may demotivate others in the team; not everyone has my drive.

Competition®

COMPETITION® for Career Success

You thrive in roles where "winning" is a key motivator. Whether in teams or on your own, having your performance measured for excellence energizes you and keeps your eyes on the prize.

According to Gallup®: People exceptionally talented in the Competition theme measure their progress against the performance of others. They strive to win first place and revel in contests.

Celebrate:

- How you embody the spirit of winning
- Winning together is as important as winning alone
- Your drive and tenacity that inspires
- Knowing where to set the bar

Evaluate:

- Am I being a sore loser?
- Is MY win becoming more important than OUR win?
- Am I setting the bar too high?
- Am I praising the effort, even if the outcome isn't as hoped?

What to look for: It is important for you to find roles in competitive industries & environments where the everyday expectation is to win and be at the top. Quotas, commissions and/or performance goals will keep you focused because you love having tangible measurements.

How to search: Determine whether you want a team to motivate or you prefer a more solitary role where you can push yourself to your personal best. Create goals for yourself to keep you motivated in the job search and perhaps talk with others in similar roles to see how they've been successful in their path. Challenge yourself to think big and reach for the stars as that will motivate you to get the best position you can.

What to communicate: You are a natural at selling yourself and why you'd be a better selection than someone else. Your energy, drive, and determination will shine and propel you into the first-place race. Talk about both "team spirit" and "individual wins" to truly achieve success.

How to succeed: Determine the measures you are aiming for early on. Be mindful that others may not share the same competitive drive that you have and ensure that there is collaboration as well as healthy competition on the team. Be sure to clearly define the metrics you'll be measured by so that you know when you've succeeded.

Sharpen your talent with these questions:

What kinds of roles have clear measurements which allow you to compare your performance to that of others?

What tools and skills give you an edge over your competitors?

How can you highlight your drive for both personal and team wins?

What standards or measurements will you use to make sure you have a winning plan?

Valeyne G, USA

Connectedness allows me to see connections in all things in my day-to-day work. Whether it's introducing colleagues to one another or seeing how projects are related, I see possibilities everywhere to bring people and things together for the greater good. Deep in my soul, I feel a connection to something larger than myself. I am constantly aware of how we are connected and assume there is a reason for everything which helps me bounce back from setbacks quickly. I need to be aware of this when supporting others so as not to minimize their struggle. This has been a driving force for me to bring compassion to colleagues, while inspiring the teams I work within to accomplish their goals. It also gives me purpose to pursue my mission, even when it gets hard. When I have decisions to make, I have learned to trust my intuition instead of procrastinating and waiting for the "right moment/time/situation". This "knowing" has helped me decide when it was time to leave an organization, say yes to a new one and even start my own business.

Connectedness®

CONNECTEDNESS® for Career Success

You thrive in environments where there is opportunity to be in community. This kind of work is both meaningful and satisfying for your soul. It's easy for you to stay motivated when your job is connected to a larger mission that you believe in.

According to Gallup®: People exceptionally talented in the Connectedness theme have faith in the links among all things. They believe there are few coincidences and that almost every event has meaning.

Celebrate:

- How you trust your inner wisdom
- Your natural compassion for all living things
- Your ability to be a bridge-builder by bringing people together
- Your desire to be a part of something bigger

Evaluate:

- Am I coming off as naive?
- Am I waiting for circumstances to be "just right" before taking action?
- Are my personal boundaries blurry?
- Am I leaving too many things to fate instead of making a decision?

What to look for: You enjoy feeling like you are a part of something larger than yourself. Whether it be more altruistic, or connected to a larger environmental or social cause, as long as you can partner with others to promote those values, you will be in your element.

How to search: You will make the most of meeting people who share your passions because you see opportunity everywhere. Stay open to possibilities as it may lead to careers you never would have considered. You handle rejection well, believing it wasn't meant to be and know another opportunity is waiting for you. You will enjoy joining professional associations and attending conferences with people who share your values.

What to communicate: Express how you bring alignment to the job through purpose, keeping diversity top of mind. Highlight for employers how previous life/work experience has naturally led to this opportunity. Speak confidently about successes and challenges, putting context around the situation, for example, "the failure to meet a sales goal indicated I was better off focusing on marketing."

How to succeed: Learn more about the organization's purpose/mission/vision and how your role contributes to it. Make connections with those who are the driving force behind the mission. Seek to understand the stakeholders in the organization and how your work connects to serving them.

Sharpen your talent with these questions:

What organizations or roles fit your mission, vision, and values?

Who do you know in my community who could connect you to work that you care about?

How can you share your personal mission and how you have effectively applied it through your work?

How do you connect what you do in your role with the larger mission of the company and your team?

Cheryl P. USA

Consistency provides me with my strong sense of fairness and love of processes. These are core to my success in a variety of careers including wildlife biologist, plant pathology research assistant, medical librarian, IT manager, and Gallup® certified strengths coach. Each of them has essential processes and standard operating procedures that are a joy for me to follow. If needed, I can easily modify processes or create new ones that others find easy to follow. A project that stands out was my ability to write detailed, but easy-to-follow documentation for our new complex identity management system processes. This system provided unique usernames, email accounts, network accounts and access to specific network resources for 25 different employee and student types.

My teams (as a member or manager) and customers always know what to expect from me, that they can depend on me, and that I will treat each of them fairly. My sense of fairness can also get me into trouble. I can see unfairness everywhere and need to remind myself that most people don't see what I see and be careful not to overreact.

Consistency®

CONSISTENCY® for Career Success

You thrive in areas where clear expectations and set ground rules are required for everyone. Stability and calm are key for you in maximizing your productivity.

According to Gallup®: People exceptionally talented in the Consistency theme are keenly aware of the need to treat people the same. They crave stable routines and clear rules and procedures that everyone can follow.

Celebrate:

- Your clear expectations
- Your fairness
- How you treat others equally
- Your ability to set clear boundaries

Evaluate:

- Am I more concerned with rules than people?
- Are rigid expectations prioritized over responding to the needs of others?
- Am I enforcing rather than discussing or understanding?
- Is my way the only way?

What to look for: It is important to find a career where regulations and rules are expected to be adhered to and followed. Leadership positions may be of particular interest as you value treating others fairly and equitably. You'll do best in an environment that allows you to have a predictable schedule or routine.

How to search: Make a list of rules or routines that are important for you to have in a job role and then research opportunities based on roles that share those traits. Certain policies or values you have may be non-negotiable in your eyes. Set up a timeline for yourself of when you'll search each week in a way that allows the search to not become overwhelming.

What to communicate: Your comfort with rules and expectations transmits confidence as well as your steady nature and clear understanding of what is required of you. Be sure to let the interviewer know that you are familiar with how the job matches your own value system.

How to succeed: Learn the policies of the company and use this to determine your fit within the organization. Be willing to occasionally step outside your comfort zone to explore new ways of doing things and potential ways to update and revise the rules.

Sharpen your talent with these questions:

What kinds of jobs require steady decision making and procedural objectives?

How do you identify organizations which are driven by equitable policies and procedures and align with your expectations?

Which of your past successes demonstrate your ability to abide by agreed upon rules and implement them fairly while still being open to innovation?

How can you understand the expectations and policies which are important to the organization's culture and success?

Lisa L, USA

Leading with Context helps me take time to find out how well things worked before. I feel best when I have a snapshot of how we got to the present moment. Looking at organizational, or departmental history helps me identify the gaps or successes that help my teams move forward and avoid mistakes. My visionary supervisors say I am a good security system. When projects and ideas are innovative, cutting edge, or in the beginning phases of development, I fail to notice the excitement and anticipation because it hasn't been vetted. I'm often wondering if these ideas already exist.

My Context has slowed down my ability to execute things quicker at work. I often feel like I need the big picture before proceeding. I rarely trust my original ideas. I will use prior projects as a blueprint for my own ideas making me less creative. I am often in my head trying to understand how everyone in the room got here knowing folks' role history helps me find ways to appreciate the work they have done.

Context®

CONTEXT® for Career Success

You thrive in roles where you can be the investigator. You enjoy researching the history of projects and opportunities which will propel projects - and people - forward by learning from the past.

According to Gallup®: People exceptionally talented in the Context theme enjoy thinking about the past. They understand the present by researching its history.

Celebrate:

- That you have a relevant, historical perspective
- Your love for the backstory
- Learning from past mistakes
- Respecting your predecessors or elders

Evaluate:

- Am I too focused on the past?
- Am I holding a grudge?
- Questioning the perspectives without trust?
- Am I resisting change?

What to look for: Consider looking for roles where you will have a chance to research, investigate or maintain traditions. You are also great at establishing frameworks around "what has been" to build "what could be".

How to search: Look at your own work history to establish where you were happiest and what you were doing. Use this knowledge to search for new opportunities which will tap into that skill set. Consider contacting past colleagues to search for new job openings as well. Research the trends in the industry and understand where emerging opportunities might exist based on what's affecting the industry today.

What to communicate: Show how you learn from the past to improve in the present both for yourself and for projects you've managed. Come to the interview armed with questions which demonstrate your ability to research and investigate, showing that you know the organization, their mission, and how you can contribute.

How to succeed: Find a mentor who will help you understand the history of both the organization and the role you are entering. This will help you decide the best course of action before jumping into action.

Sharpen your talent with these questions:

What kinds of things do you like to research and investigate?

How can you learn about the history of others who are on a similar career path to discover new opportunities for yourself?

Which stories from your past are most relevant to the current role you are interviewing for?

How can you learn about the company's history and what has worked well in the past?

Justin D, USA

As a general surgery resident preparing for complex fellowship interviews, I carefully researched every program and learned about the surgeons I would potentially be working with. I read medical journal articles written by each one and listened to past interviews to understand who they were. I anticipated our commonalities and what they might be concerned with as they interviewed me.

It's the same care I take when preparing for an operation and interacting with a family whose loved one needs cancer treatment. Prior to meeting for the first time, I am meticulous in my review of the medical record. I decide on the appropriate therapy and carefully consider all risks involved with resection. When I meet them, I deliberately lay out the operative plan and discuss everything that might go wrong during and after their operation. I always take my time, explaining every detail and how we plan to mitigate potential challenges. I take the time to answer all their questions and address their concerns to the best of my ability. On the day of their operation, I have already re-reviewed their chart and imaging, am methodical in the way I carefully remove affected tissues and continuously anticipate challenges and ways to mitigate them to ensure better outcomes for the patient. When I explained this in my interview, I earned a spot in my top choice fellowship.

Deliberative®

DELIBERATIVE® for Career Success

You thrive in roles where you can pair your cautious approach with careful decision-making and show those around you how to evaluate risks thoroughly. Your thoughtful actions translate into a sense of stability and protection.

According to Gallup®: People exceptionally talented in the Deliberative theme are best described by the serious care they take in making decisions or choices. They anticipate obstacles.

Celebrate:

- Your vigilance
- Your perspective from multiple points of view
- Your conscientiousness
- You measure risk carefully and move forward accordingly

Evaluate:

- Am I too afraid of making the wrong decision?
- Am I playing Devil's Advocate just to be contrary?
- Am I holding others back with my cautiousness?
- Am I unwilling to trust decisions to others?

What to look for: Any role where risk evaluation is part of the job requirement will likely be a great fit for you. Having time to evaluate and analyze projects is also a necessity, so consider something that allows for a measured approach rather than quick pivots.

How to search: You are already keenly aware of the potential risks of seeking a new job or position. Evaluate the pros and cons of the roles and/or companies you are considering which will ensure you have a greater comfort level at the interview stage.

What to communicate: Consider doing a mock interview with someone to help you thoughtfully prepare for the questions ahead of time. Think of the difficult questions that might be asked of you and how you would answer them. Show how when you take action, you have guaranteed the best possible outcome by taking calculated risks.

How to succeed: Let your team know you enjoy having some time to consider your possibilities before taking action. Ask for clear deadlines and expectations for yourself and others so you can move forward comfortably and on time.

Sharpen your talent with these questions:

What kinds of roles allow you to take time in making careful decisions and meet your level of risk tolerance?

Which jobs will make the most of your ability to see obstacles and plan for them?

How can you communicate the value of evaluating obstacles before taking action?

How do you trust others to make informed decisions beyond your scope?

Sonny L. USA

In 40 years as a football coach, I never fired a person. Instead, I took extra time to talk with them and steer them in the right direction to improve. I always believed we could get the most out of our players by spending time with them and I'd tell them, "I know you can get the job done for us." Coaching is teaching. You don't see the person for who they are, you see them for who they can become. I did that by studying the playbooks of some of the most successful coaches. I went to clinics and I sent my coaches and players to clinics so they could learn from the best. I'd even have other coaches come and watch and give me advice so that I developed as a coach. I always knew we could win if we got the most out of each player and coach - and we did win but that wasn't our focus. Winning is a by-product of developing people.

Developer®

DEVELOPER® for Career Success

You thrive in roles where you have the chance to encourage and cultivate the special abilities of those around you. You are able to celebrate each unique step in the journey of others, recognizing that every step is a step forward.

According to Gallup®: People exceptionally talented in the Developer theme recognize and cultivate the potential in others. They spot the signs of each small improvement and derive satisfaction from evidence of progress.

Celebrate:

- Your dedication to progress
- Your talent spotting skills
- Your patience
- Your belief in the potential of others

Evaluate:

- Are we making progress?
- Is this worthy of my time?
- Is the other person interested in developing themselves?
- Am I pushing too hard?

What to look for: It is important for you to find roles which will allow you to mentor others and be a catalyst for their success. You enjoy building interpersonal relationships and having a direct impact on the professional development of those around you. You'll appreciate organizations that provide opportunities for your own professional development.

How to search: Consider a coach or mentor to help you in your own development, one who can help you recognize the best path of growth for your professional goals and will take an interest in seeing you accomplish what you set out to do. Consider becoming part of a professional organization or sign up for training to foster your own career development while you prepare for what is next.

What to communicate: Recount past successes where you have facilitated the growth of others and what the process looked like. Showcase your own potential by showing how you have grown in your own career and what led you here today.

How to succeed: Build relationships early on with your team by asking questions about their career goals and what they hope to achieve and how they want to grow. Show interest by asking how you might help them reach their goals.

Sharpen your talent with these questions:

Which roles offer you the opportunity to supervise, train, teach, or mentor others?

Where can you find a mentor that will help me explore roles in both for-profit and nonprofit organizations?

Which stories best showcase your ability to see and nurture the potential in others?

How can you tap into opportunities to both mentor and be mentored as well as explore professional development and training for yourself?

My Discipline has influenced my career choices greatly, including how I work. I've mainly been in recruitment and executive search, after it was pointed out to me that it's fundamentally about excellent processes! I briefly worked in organisational development but found it was too unstructured and didn't lend itself to my strengths as well. Discipline is more than just a tidy desk and being up to date with my filing. It's my ability to create and follow systems and processes, keeping order for the team as well as for my clients -making sure that "t's are crossed, and i's are dotted".

In practice my work runs smoothly and there are very few last-minute emergencies. I have a clear picture of my commitments and deadlines ensuring my work is delivered ahead of schedule. Discipline enables me to be a proactive communicator, as I have lists of who I need to call and email.

Over time I've realised that these behaviours won't come easily to someone without Discipline. I've learned to be patient and to be very clear around what I need and by when. I've helped my team by creating checklists and flowcharts for them to use and making sure we stick to them.

Discipline®

DISCIPLINE® for Career Success

You thrive in environments where structure and routine are the order of the day. You are motivated to keep track of the details and schedules ensuring that everyone stays on task.

According to Gallup®: People exceptionally talented in the Discipline theme enjoy routine and structure. Their world is best described by the order they create.

Celebrate:

- How you easily break down big tasks
- Your ease with efficiency
- Your attention to detail
- Your ability to maintain a routine or schedule

Evaluate:

- Am I too rigid with others?
- Am I willing to be flexible when necessary?
- Am I too hard on others with their inattention to detail?
- Am I unwilling to change?

What to look for: It is important for you to find roles where you can keep order for yourself and those around you. You'll appreciate being in an environment with a clear structure or one that values the structure you can bring and one in which follow-through is highly appreciated.

How to search: Creating a routine will keep you focused. Schedule out your to-do list for applications, interviews and contacts to make. Look for resources which spell out the process of how to implement a job search plan and follow it step-by-step. Set deadlines for each step in the process.

What to communicate: Be sure to highlight your organizational and time management skills. Showcase how you have brought order from chaos, implemented clear structure and guidelines, and/or set new procedures which helped make your team or organization more effective and productive.

How to succeed: Give yourself time to plan and observe the rhythm in the office and the structure of how to work best with your colleagues. It may differ from your normal routine, but once you understand how they work, you will be able to find your own rhythm and get to work.

Sharpen your talent with these questions:

What routines or schedules are important for you to be at your best and which roles accommodate that?

How could you set up a daily schedule that effectively tackles the most pressing tasks?

What story demonstrates how you've created structures that led to a successful outcome?

How can you contribute to the goals of the company by bringing structure and organization while also staying open to current structures in place?

Bari R, USA

What I most love to do in my work is connect with people - I love to hear their "stories"! I work in international development and my main focus on designing and facilitating learning activities. I use my Empathy in my work all the time. I channel how learners may be feeling about the topic (bored? intimidated? intrigued?), which helps me choose the right activities to engage them. I've also been told I have the ability to "read a room". I sense how people are feeling which helps me interpret what's going on and provides clues on what approach to take for the best outcome. Being empathetic also helps me build trust with others. I've been able to really internalize the value of a team: each team member's unique contribution. I am now able to appreciate the unique value my empathy can add to a team dynamic or an organization.

Heightened Empathy can also impact and stall my decision making. I naturally scan my mind for the different ways it could impact those involved. If I anticipate a potential negative outcome, I want to mitigate that impact or I begin to second-guess taking the step at all. I realize I'm looking for an approach which works for everyone and that's not always possible.

Empathy®

EMPATHY® for Career Success

You thrive in roles which allow you to give input on the overall culture, the emotional wellbeing of team members, and have a service-oriented mission. you have an incredible capacity to hold space for others.

According to Gallup®: People exceptionally talented in the Empathy theme can sense other people's feelings by imagining themselves in others' lives or situations.

Celebrate:

- Feeling what others are feeling
- How you can "read a room"
- Expressing your emotions with ease
- Your kindness

Evaluate:

- Am I taking on the feelings of others too personally?
- Do I express my feelings adequately and appropriately?
- Am I being taken advantage of by others?
- Do I have clear boundaries?

What to search for: Look for opportunities that will allow you to connect emotionally with people in a meaningful way. Pay attention to opportunities where noticing what others are feeling is part of the job. Service oriented organizations and projects will motivate you greatly.

How to search: Researching a company's culture will be important for you. Find a partner who will help you stay focused. Think about how you meet the needs of others and make a list of organizations that serve people you would love to serve. Connect with others who are making a difference in a similar space. And most importantly, listen to your gut and what it tells you about the opportunity.

What to communicate: Display your strong interpersonal skills. Tell stories of how noticing others' needs helped you meet them; or the value of your intuition when developing successful projects, teams, or saying the right thing to encourage others. Pay attention to your body language and that of the interviewer as your non-verbal skills are strong and can make a big impact.

How to succeed: You will connect quickly with others on your team, and your ability to listen will create a safe and trusting environment. Your ability to be vulnerable will prove your interest in connecting on a deeper level. Remember, some might require a bit more time to share, so give them the space they need to connect with you.

Sharpen your talent with these questions:

What organizations offer the best cultural fit for you?

Who can help you identify supervisors or teams with whom you will connect and support as a valuable partner?

How can you best display how your intuition has served you and those around you in a positive way?

How might others experience having a new coworker differently than you might?

Rene R, USA

Focus is a pretty consistent thread throughout my life. I tend to set goals which may appear to others as lofty and difficult to attain. Ex. 1: With the odds against me and INS officials laughing at my intention, I successfully immigrated to the US from Germany after 2 years of persistent effort. Ex. 2: At a startup, I had both leadership responsibilities while also juggling multiple critical projects at the same time. While challenging, Focus allowed me to effectively divide my attention into 30-45 min chunks, so I could dive deep into project A and make progress before immersing myself in the next project. This technique of shifting deep focus allowed me to juggle all these balls and stay in control.

For me, it creates a certain tenacity that allows me to succeed under difficult circumstances. I make it a habit to regularly zoom out from the minutiae of tasks and deliverables to review progress against the overall goal and make adjustments. If certain tasks don't help me achieve goals and seem wasteful, I get rid of them.

I also recognize it can be hard to really relax as I need to feel consistently productive. Also, delays bother me, especially if they seem to be caused by others not being organized or focused.

Focus®

FOCUS® for Career Success

You thrive in environments where there are clear cut objectives and you are able to keep your eye on the target, prioritize your tasks, hit the deadlines, and accomplish the goals.

According to Gallup®: People exceptionally talented in the Discipline theme enjoy routine and structure. Their world is best described by the order they create.

Celebrate:

- Your ability to prioritize tasks
- Your targeted drive
- Your ability to zero-in on important details
- Your concentration superpower

Evaluate:

- Am I too focused on the details to see the big picture?
- Am I placing my priorities over the needs of others?
- Am I listening closely enough to others who might not have the same goals?
- Are my goals more important than people?

What to look for: You most appreciate being in an organization or project that has a well-defined outcome and expectations. It's important for you to be able to focus on the outcome as well as being able to have some autonomy over the prioritization of tasks.

How to search: Identify your career goals and break it down in the steps you need to get there. You are good at achieving your short-term goals to achieve your overall career objectives. Outline all the tasks you must accomplish in your search and take action based on the priority.

What to communicate: Highlight how you accomplish things efficiently, and that you need little supervision since you can stay on track and are not easily distracted. You excel at describing your long-term goals and the steps you will take to get there. Draw from your experience with staying motivated to accomplish complex tasks to demonstrate your follow through. Be sure to see the overall type of job you want rather than just the specifics of only one job.

How to succeed: You will be noticed as you begin to accomplish new tasks; however, keep in mind to delegate when possible and to work as a team. Though you are deeply focused on tackling your list, be sure to socialize and take time to meet your new colleagues as well.

Sharpen your talent with these questions:

Which roles allow you to have control over the prioritization of tasks and a direct impact on the outcome?

How can you best align your short-term goals with your overall objectives?

Which experiences or tasks demonstrate your ability to maintain focus on the details while still delivering on big picture goals?

How can you share your need for focused work time as well as learn to whom you can delegate specific tasks?

Maria Y, *MBA, PHR, GCDF,* USA

You can call me a dreamer. Even as a little girl I told everyone that I would be successful, live in the Western world, own a mansion, and get married to a prince. Not all of that happened but the drive is still there! The future was always on my mind.

Understanding my strengths made choosing my career easier. I transitioned from Finance to HR, starting early because of my Futuristic strength. Having a well-visioned plan, I landed the HR career I wanted, obtained my certification, and continue to grow in the field that I love. As an HR professional, I am always thinking and working towards process and operational improvements, employee advocacy in terms of improving retention and engagement, equity and justice.

I also own and operate a braiding store in Colorado which serves our community and our neighbors in Wyoming and Nebraska. It is the only one of its kind in the area. I consistently search for ways to improve and grow. Today I am so happy living my dreams...In the Western world, in a career I love and continue to grow, owning a business, co-instructing part-time while sharing my stories and building my dream house! I always have the future in mind and working towards it!

Futuristic®

FUTURISTIC® for Career Success

You thrive in environments which allow you to dream, share your visions and work toward a common goal. You are energized by "tomorrow" and "what if" scenarios which allow your imagination to explore all the possibilities.

According to Gallup®: People exceptionally talented in the Futuristic theme are inspired by the future and what could be. They energize others with their visions of the future.

Celebrate:

- Your creativity and imagination
- Your vision for a better tomorrow
- The ability to see possibility instead of roadblocks
- Your ability to dream big

Evaluate:

- Am I appreciating the here and now?
- Am I being realistic with my vision of the future?
- Am I remembering to say thank you or appreciate current efforts?
- Am I co-creating with others or am I telling others how it should be?

What to look for: You enjoy being part of an organization which focuses on innovation, imagination, and a vision for tomorrow. In a start-up, you have the ability to shape the overall purpose, vision, and mission of the company as it begins. In a more established company, it will be important that you align with the vision they already have and how you can support it.

How to search: Look for opportunities which allow you to help the organization plan and conceptualize new ideas and strategies. You can be a big part of new innovations both now and well down the road. Picture the new position and how it would impact yourself and your family.

What to communicate: Focus on your transferable skills and how they will be valuable to an employer. You excel at imagining and explaining what you will do in the potential job. Using "I will" or "I imagine" shows off your strength; however, remember to also focus on how your past experiences apply and make you a great candidate. Talk about how you envision the future of this role when you interview.

How to succeed: You inspire others to think of ways to be innovative and not be complacent. Try to find out from seasoned employees as much as you can about the company's past tactics so you can best craft approaches that haven't already been tried. Focus on follow-through that will make your imagined future achievable.

Sharpen your talent with these questions:

What excites you about the future and which industries fuel that passion?

How can you identify roles which position you well for the future you envision?

What kind of vision do you have for yourself in this role and where it might lead?

With whom can you discuss what the team is doing now and how it's connected to where you all want to be in 5 years?

Shannon K-M, USA

My Harmony likes to look for and facilitate consensus. I am often known as the peacekeeper, but I remain neutral and can easily see both sides of a situation. While some people with Harmony might avoid conflict, I personally like to insert myself right in it to help others come to a resolution. This serves me well in my role as a Talent and Learning Consultant and is often focused on team building. Given I see both sides, one watchout is that others may perceive me as defending someone, when really my intent is to assume positive intent in others. I also like closure and to ensure people are okay and able to productively work together and get along.

Sometimes making decisions can be tough since I don't want to unnecessarily rock the boat. I find it helpful to advocate when I feel strongly about something. And when I don't, to be clear about that, so others don't perceive me as being indecisive. I can also be overly accommodating, being a people pleaser and concerned with what others think. At the end of the day, a job in which people work productively together with open communication suits my Harmony quite well.

Harmony®

HARMONY® for Career Success

You thrive in environments where there is a high collaborative focus and low competition among co-workers. You are also a natural mediator and serve well in situations where an objective third party is required.

According to Gallup®: People exceptionally talented in the Harmony theme look for consensus. They don't enjoy conflict; rather, they seek areas of agreement.

Celebrate:

- Your calm and balanced nature
- Your ability to gain consensus
- Seeing reciprocity as a win-win and it's not always 50/50
- Your negotiating skills

Evaluate:

- Am I avoiding conflict?
- Am I just 'people pleasing'?
- Am I being truthful or evasive to keep the peace?
- Am I being indecisive?

What to look for: It's important to consider opportunities where you can use your natural conflict resolution ability to find common ground, especially where people or relationships are involved. Also consider that the company culture and how colleagues work together as collaborators is a key factor for your overall peace of mind and success. You'll thrive in a collaborative, positive environment.

How to search: Work with people who are supportive in the job search as this will increase your confidence. Maintain peace within yourself and with others throughout the job search, knowing that while it may be competitive, you will find the right position for you. Remain open-minded to various career paths.

What to communicate: Highlight your ability to create calm and peace in any group. Share your ability to identify what people have in common, which enables you to help them to consistently reach an agreement. Show what a valuable contribution you would be to the team, by using your ease of sensing what the interviewers are looking for; however, be sure to verbalize your own feelings and values as well.

How to succeed: Take an interest in your new co-workers so you can identify collaborative partners and establish trusting relationships. Keep in mind to initiate tasks and ideas rather than just following along with others. Offer to gather people to work together. Look for common ground at every opportunity.

Sharpen your talent with these questions:

Do you prefer roles which focus on conflict resolution or are you more drawn to a fully collaborative environment? Consider what attracts you to that environment.

Who would be a helpful search partner for you and how could they best support you?

How has your ability to resolve conflict or negotiate compromise helped you succeed?

How can you use your talent to bring team members together?

Wendy W, USA

My high Ideation means I am never at a loss for possibility. When the team is searching for options, I have the capacity to provide what feels like limitless alternatives. Now, they may not all be plausible, but that isn't the point. I've learned sometimes we need to generate lots of ideas to give us the best chance for finding the one that succeeds. My ideas can bring fresh perspectives that prompt new ways of considering the problem, equipping us to move toward better solutions. Of course, there may be reasons why my Ideation can get blocked — illness, stress, anxiety, for example — but once those are addressed, I can freely tap into the river of ideas once again. In fact, taking time to think about ideas, and then capture the best ones to refine later, energizes me and makes me feel good.

Ideation®

IDEATION® for Career Success

You thrive in environments that provide the freedom to express your ideas and creativity. Brainstorming is your superpower and requires a space where it is valued and appreciated.

According to Gallup®: People exceptionally talented in the Ideation theme are fascinated by ideas. They are able to find connections between seemingly disparate phenomena.

Celebrate:

- Your love of brainstorming
- Making connections others may overlook
- Your ability to innovate
- Asking "why not?" instead of "why?"

Evaluate:

- Are my ideas actionable?
- Do I change direction too fast?
- Am I delaying the end goal?
- Am I communicating my ideas effectively?

What to look for: You need a creative and flexible space, where your ideas can flow and "Why not?" is more valued than "Why?" Rigid structures or ways of thinking will feel too constricting. Look for the working environment where your ideas will be valued, and you'll have freedom to explore possibilities.

How to search: Use your talent to imagine various ways to reach your long-term goals. Your creativity helps you stand out from other candidates and in finding hidden job opportunities. Think outside the box for related industries and roles you can pivot to.

What to communicate: Spotlight your ingenuity, resourcefulness, and motivation to learn new principles and concepts. Bring high energy and fresh answers to questions about how you would contribute to the company more than other candidates. Consider brainstorming in mock interviews to fully develop some of your ideas as some employers might not be able to "connect the dots" of an interesting but incomplete idea.

How to succeed: Because you can think of many different ways to execute a plan, achieve a goal, or present an idea, remember to conscientiously choose a means by which to accomplish these tasks, and then follow through to keep from getting stuck in the idea and planning stage. Volunteer to be part of entrepreneurial ventures or projects that would benefit from your creativity.

Sharpen your talent with these questions:

What kinds of roles would celebrate your quick thinking and high creativity?

How can you generate ideas to find opportunities that might be currently off your radar?

What are some unusual solutions or ideas you've had that ended up being a big success?

Who can you brainstorm with before meetings so you can enter when a clear focus is needed?

Kathy E, USA

I've always been an includer—as a kid I drew in groups of mismatched friends; in college I'd bring a diverse group of people together in the clubs and organizations I led; in my friend and family circles I am the party-thrower. For the past 20+ years I've been a non-profit leader working in the margins of life and faith. My current role as the co-founder and community cultivator of The Refuge, a hub for healing community, social action, and creative collaboration is the best culmination of this strength and brings me such joy. I have the honor and privilege to gather a wild mix of people across socioeconomics, demographics, beliefs, ages and life experiences. We host gatherings, support groups, special events, and workshops, each and every one of which includes people who would normally not come together. Witnessing someone who lives outside sitting eating, laughing and sharing stories with someone who makes six figures, a single mom and her kids, and an LGBTQ+ teen, I can't help but smile. As a leader, I intentionally ensure that every team has an empty seat available for someone who wants to serve. I create space in every gathering for every voice to be heard, It's beautiful but also messy! It can also be hard. I want **everyone** to be able to play, which can make things too complicated, inefficient, and sometimes frustrating to others.

Includer®

INCLUDER® for Career Success

You thrive in environments which allow you to be part of a group or team. Being a team leader is something you may enjoy since you easily create a feeling of togetherness.

According to Gallup®: People exceptionally talented in the Includer theme accept others. They show awareness of those who feel left out and make an effort to include

Celebrate:

- Your abilities as a natural team builder
- Making others feel at ease, especially new people
- Your acceptance of others as they are
- How you fight for or support the underdog

Evaluate:

- Am I being indecisive?
- Am I avoiding confrontation?
- Am I including the *right* people for the task at hand?
- Am I being overly generous?

What to look for: Consider roles and opportunities that allow you to actively participate in a team environment or even build teams for projects and/or departments. Working with groups of people who normally feel excluded is another area in which you would find enjoyment and satisfaction.

How to search: Build a network and get energized by finding peers who will conduct a job search with you. The team setting within the job search makes the process more enjoyable. Interview or shadow professionals who are currently in jobs that interest you to get a sense of their daily responsibilities; the personal interaction can help you narrow down your options. Consider joining a job search support group.

What to communicate: Demonstrate your open-mindedness to people who share different perspectives. Talk about team building and enhancing workplace positivity using examples from your past roles. While focusing and including others is a strong suit, remember to add how you individually contributed to goals and accomplishments.

How to succeed: Balance your desire to make your co-workers always feel a part of things - which boosts morale, teamwork, and productivity - by also spending enough energy focused on your own individual tasks. Find a way to join affinity groups or become involved in a community in your new work setting.

Sharpen your talent with these questions:

Who are the people you most enjoy working with and in what capacity?

What are the top industries you'd most like to work in and who might you know who could create an introduction for you?

What makes you great at building diverse teams, bringing all voices to the table, and how does this make a positive impact?

Where can you get involved in both work and/or extra-curricular activities to improve your connection with your co-workers?

James R, USA

I find seeing the unique talents, capabilities, and qualities of each person comes naturally. I use this strength as a people and project manager to connect and learn about individuals and groups and to get things done. Individualization helps me identify and gather the right people together, at the right time, so we can solve important business problems and overcome obstacles.

There are challenges to having this strength, and I must prevent myself from relying solely on my interpretation of individuals by countering my intuitive understanding with facts and evidence.

Becoming aware of this strength has empowered me to find ways to maximize it in every interaction, which has made me a better manager and leader. It has also helped me better understand myself and how my unique combination of strengths is not only a source of professional power but the essence of my personal brand.

Individualization®

INDIVIDUALIZATION® for Career Success

> *You thrive in roles which give you the opportunity to make a personal impact and give recognition to others. You excel when you can help others realize and act upon their potential.*

According to Gallup®: People exceptionally talented in the Individualization theme are intrigued with the unique qualities of each person. They have a gift for figuring out how different people can work together productively

Celebrate:

- You celebrate the unique individuality and differences of each person
- How you make others feel special
- Recognizing all the factors which create the 'whole' person
- Your personalized attention

Evaluate:

- Is the group being sacrificed for the individual?
- Am I valuing potential over performance?
- Are the rules too flexible?
- Am I being too flexible – bending to the desires/needs of others?

What to look for: You do well in roles which allow for both you - and those around you - to do what they do best. Look for roles where you can customize how you work with people and delegate work based on individual talents. While public recognition may not be necessary, a culture which recognizes the value you provide will go a long way in your well-being and staying positive on the job.

How to search: Reflect on the unique fit between who you are and what you do with your life. You are motivated to find a job that matches your personality and purpose. Make a chart listing specific differences in each position, ways in which you uniquely fit the role, and network with those directly in the same industry - customizing your requests or interactions based on who they are.

What to communicate: Talk confidently about your own values, as well as how you understand the specific needs and talents of others. Articulate how the job is uniquely a good fit for you and how you contribute to the goals of the organization. Become an expert in describing your own talents and style, while showing you have a talent for spotting the potential of others.

How to succeed: Build relationships with your co-workers as you take note of the things that are important to each of them. Remember to check in about their roles and projects, as well as get to know them on a personal level. This will serve you well by knowing who to go to for assistance and who will most efficiently complete a task.

Sharpen your talent with these questions:

What unique characteristics does your dream company or role possess?

Who can make personal introductions for you to jobs for which you have applied or have interest?

How can you highlight what makes your contribution unique?

How can you personalize your own tasks while serving the shared goals of your team?

Carol P, USA

As a Professional Résumé Writer, I routinely engage with clients who are either currently employed in, or searching for, a position that lies somewhere within every industry and job function imaginable – many of which I am unfamiliar with. Throughout each project, my INPUT strength drives me to do "deep-dive" research into cited occupations, companies & organizations, job titles, competencies, etc., to familiarize myself with the client's occupational world. In turn, the knowledge I gain enables me to reflect accurately and, in numerous cases, explain the significance and connection of the client's past experiences to a potential job fit through the writing of their résumé, cover letter, and online (LinkedIn) profile. Utilizing my Input strength is a key differentiator in my approach to telling one's professional story – I can confidently work with an occupationally diverse client base and express learned knowledge within their career documents. Input LOVES Output!

Input®

INPUT® for Career Success

You thrive in environments which will allow you to research innovative ideas or find new ways of doing things and then sharing what you know with others. You are a master resourcer.

According to Gallup®: People exceptionally talented in the Input theme have a need to collect and archive. They may accumulate information, ideas, artifacts or even relationships.

Celebrate:

- Your resourcefulness
- Your desire to share information & resources
- Having the right information, at the right time, for the right person
- Your better than average memory

Evaluate:

- Am I asking too many questions?
- Am I applying what I'm learning?
- Am I collecting things which have a purpose?
- Am I oversharing information?

What to look for: Look for opportunities which allow you to surround yourself with new knowledge and offer you the opportunity to develop creative approaches to situations or problems. You find it rewarding to be in a position as a topic expert. You'll do best in roles that require you to gather information or research regularly.

How to search: Collect information on jobs that interest you and organize what you find in a way that helps you prioritize which jobs are the best fit. You might also want to crowdsource information with peers or other experts to help you make a decision.

What to communicate: Share how you are able to be a resource because of your ability to gather information and talk about your ability to relay this information to facilitate growth, tackle projects, or meet goals. Use the information from the research you conducted during your job search and pick out key words that seem important to interviewers. Keeping track of your past experiences, strengths, and weaknesses will give you more information to draw from during the interview.

How to succeed: Your ability to catalog and remember information gathered in meetings and conversations may be helpful as you begin projects and assignments. It will also help you share your resources with your team members, ensuring they have what they need to do their job well. Know that you can move forward even if you don't have all the information you might want to have.

Sharpen your talent with these questions:

What/Who is the most important beneficiary of your knowledge and resources?

What resources do you already have that will help you with your job search?

Which story best shows how you expertly manage to acquire and use tools, resources, and information that have practical and transferable utility?

How can you understand the resources already available to you and what might still be needed?

Sumarie P, S. Africa

Intellection is the biggest reason that my mind never stops running. My mind has never been a restful blank. It is just always going. Sometimes slower, but never completely at a standstill. People would often compliment my insight into matters and if I think about it, it probably comes from the fact that I am always molding information and ideas in my mind. The insight just sort of happens; I don't really work at it. And that to me is the miracle of strengths – it just happens, almost effortlessly.

I created a 12-week leadership development course from scratch - all in my mind! After I have been thinking about it and tweaking it in my mind for about 3 months, I put it together in a few days. Because by then it was pretty well thought through.

The one thing about Intellection that can be frustrating is that I regularly need time to process. And others don't always understand it, so they think there is something wrong if I take off to be alone with my thoughts. I am quite dependent on those alone times. Without it everything tends to fall apart.

Intellection®

INTELLECTION® for Career Success

You thrive in environments which allow for in-depth discussion with colleagues and where sharing ideas is encouraged. Asking deep questions and having time to think things through is a "must have" for you.

According to Gallup®: People exceptionally talented in the Intellection theme are characterized by their intellectual activity. They are introspective and appreciate intellectual discussions.

Celebrate:

- Your depth and profoundness for understanding
- Your philosopher's mindset
- Having deep, meaningful conversations
- Your ability to move slowly

Evaluate:

- Am I isolating myself?
- Am I thinking about the right things?
- Am I getting frustrated with others who move faster than I do?
- Am I building walls or emotional barriers to keep others at arm's length?

What to look for: Look for opportunities which allow you to have deep conversations and share ideas and perspectives in a non-judgmental environment. You enjoy talking at length with others and exploring their thoughts and opinions. You also need time to reflect and be alone while you make your decisions or process what you've learned.

How to search: Make a list of questions you would like to have answered and reach out to people in the career field or company for insights as you search. Consider making a timeline for your search so you can see your progress and keep moving forward. Think of what might be asked ahead of time to prepare your answers before the interview, perhaps doing practice interviews with peers or a coach.

What to communicate: You will impress with your ability to ask thoughtful and insightful questions. Because you've practiced your answers, you will come across as prepared and articulate. Let them know you will appreciate having time to consider their offer in order to make the best decision possible.

How to succeed: Your ability to ask thought-provoking questions may come across as a challenge but could eventually lead to changes which will have a positive impact creating higher productivity and efficiency. You can also use your ability to ask questions to get to know your colleagues beyond a superficial connection. Find others who enjoy discussing ideas.

Sharpen your talent with these questions:

What kinds of challenges in the world would you enjoy working on?

What are you genuinely curious about when you think about potential new careers or companies?

What story demonstrates how your ability to discuss big ideas/ask hard questions made a positive difference in the workplace?

What are you genuinely interested to know about your coworkers or new company and who can you interact with to learn more?

Susan C, USA

My natural curiosity and love for learning translated into pursuing formal degrees, certifications and actively seeking the next learning opportunity to grow in my career or to gain expertise in my field. As a result, I took several career pivots in the search for new challenges. I transitioned from counseling and social work to a career in Human Resources and readily went back to school to get my HR certification. When I got laid off from HR, I took the opportunity to seek out a new challenge and ventured into career and executive coaching. I embraced attending trainings and getting coaching certifications. For me, the downside of Learner has been keeping myself challenged and finding new opportunities for growth. This has at times made me quick to leave a job or career in search of the satisfaction that comes with continued learning.

Learner®

LEARNER® for Career Success

You thrive in environments where you can continuously be exposed to new information and experiences and can share what you learn with others. You value environments that prioritize training and development.

According to Gallup®: People exceptionally talented in the Learner theme have a great desire to learn and want to continuously improve. The process of learning, rather than the outcome, excites them.

Celebrate:

- Your curiosity about many things
- Your great perspective on a variety of subjects
- Your appreciation for different ways of learning
- Learning from your mistakes

Evaluate:

- Is this just curiosity or does it serve a purpose?
- Am I a know-it-all?
- Am I applying what I learn?
- Am I sharing and/or using my knowledge appropriately?

What to look for: Look for opportunities which allow you to develop yourself and/or others as this will increase your engagement on the job. You will also enjoy researching new methods or finding new resources in order to improve company culture, products or team members, depending on your area of interest.

How to search: Make connections with others who have done what you hope to do so you can learn from them. You will enjoy being educated by their experiences. You are motivated to do the research and find creative opportunities to put your talents to work. Consider completing a certification in your industry as a demonstration of your learning.

What to communicate: Express your enthusiasm for taking on new challenges and learning new concepts. Share stories of how your ability to learn kept you on the cutting edge in your field. You can showcase your research skills by asking specific questions about the company and the role you hope to fill. This will set you apart from other candidates.

How to succeed: You will appreciate having a productive one-on-one with your new supervisor so you can quickly understand the expectations of your role and daily the ins and outs of both the team and the position. Research the industry and the company. Your curiosity will also help you get to know your colleagues better and create productive and lasting connections.

Sharpen your talent with these questions:

Which opportunities have the best development tracks for you?

What are the key tasks or responsibilities in your ideal job?

What new experience or information have you found that directly impacted a project or goal?

How can you actively apply what you've learned about the company and your coworkers to have a positive start in your new role?

Rachel M, USA

Maximizer has the power of excellence while having an edge of overdoing it! It has propelled me to greater heights than I ever imagined. When aiming Maximizer to near-perfect performance, in some cases, I've had to defend it by clarifying the needs of very important projects where excellence shouldn't be compromised. In other cases, I've had to regulate it. Where maximizing excellence could take a large investment of time to nitpick every detail, I've used other strengths to help me say, "No, this is fine or good enough (for now)." My Maximizer doesn't like to start from scratch. It is best activated when I can invest a little time researching best practices, reviewing existing methodologies or having an outstanding model that will allow me to make it even better.

Maximizer®

MAXIMIZER® for Career Success

You thrive in environments which allow you to set the pace, build on existing processes or programs to improve them, or to develop the strengths of others so they may serve in their own excellence.

According to Gallup®: People exceptionally talented in the Maximizer theme focus on strengths as a way to stimulate personal and group excellence. They seek to transform something strong into something superb.

Celebrate:

- Your dedication to excellence
- Preferring quality over quantity
- Your focus on strengths
- Your motivational manner

Evaluate:

- Am I being a perfectionist?
- Is the outcome realistic?
- Are my expectations too high?
- Am I mirroring excellence or only demanding it?

What to look for: Look for opportunities which allow you to improve yourself and those around you. You enjoy making things more efficient and improving existing systems. You prefer not to start from scratch, but rather improve upon what's already in place. You like being asked for your feedback and making the most of existing resources or doing more than was expected.

How to search: Make the most of your resume, tailoring it and improving it each time for the roles you seek and the feedback you receive from potential employers or coaches. Check in with people already successful in the roles you hope to fill and learn from their expertise.

What to communicate: Demonstrate your ability to seek excellence in both yourself and others. Talk about projects where you were able to streamline or build upon past successes to create something even better. Your passion will show through your concrete answers and your desire to deliver in a way that exceeds expectations.

How to succeed: You easily see the best in your co-workers and in your new role. This will drive you to inspire others to rise to their own potential. Remember, others may not quite be ready to rise to your vision for them, so meet them where they are and help them along the way.

Sharpen your talent with these questions:

Where can you see potential to make an impact by improving and building upon existing structures?

How can you better use existing resources to a greater extent?

How can you highlight the value of your talent with procedures, projects and/or people?

How can you effectively and efficiently aim each team member's talents?

Jennifer V, USA

As a career coach, my Positivity allows me to encourage people and get them excited about all the possibilities that exist. I think of positivity in my work as contagious enthusiasm, and I can tell it helps people think more optimistically.

Helping people understand their strengths is a natural way of leveraging Positivity. It is seeing the good in people and focusing on it and helping them focus on it too. It is also what allows me to get people talking about their strengths in interviews and stay positive about what they bring.

Positivity can be misunderstood, and people sometimes see it as not being realistic or being too focused on big dreams and not on what is accessible. But it helps me think bigger than others can and encourage others to dream too, so my clients often go for bigger outcomes than they originally thought they could.

I read somewhere that optimistic people tend to run late because they are always so sure nothing will go wrong that they don't plan for anything to. This is a blind spot of Positivity, but overall people benefit from the encouragement and the focus on silver linings it brings.

Positivity®

POSITIVITY® for Career Success

You thrive in organizations which see solutions over problems, promote a convivial and friendly culture, and allow you to be the cheerleader for those around you. You are a natural promoter.

According to Gallup®: People exceptionally talented in the Positivity theme have contagious enthusiasm. They are upbeat and can get others excited about what they are going to do.

Celebrate:

- Your 'silver-lining' attitude
- The ability to visualize a positive outcome
- Your abundance of gratitude and compliments
- Your infectious smile

Evaluate:

- Am I avoiding problems?
- Am I being naive?
- Am I complimenting with sincerity?
- Am I actively seeking positive outcomes?

What to look for: Look for opportunities which allow you to work in a team and be in a friendly work environment. Any career that allows you to encourage others and face challenges with an affirmative attitude will be rewarding. Opportunities which allow you to see possibilities rather than barriers will motivate you most.

How to search: Stay grounded and realistic in your search. While you will see benefits in many opportunities or roles, be conscious of whether it really fits your values, skills and personality. The good news is, even in rejection, you see each opportunity as a learning experience. Look for ways to encourage others, be a constructive contributor to discussions, and promote ideas in a way that gets you noticed.

What to communicate: Your high energy and upbeat outlook will easily demonstrate your positive spirit. This shows both confidence and authentic excitement about the job opportunity. Remember to show a balance of realism and optimism during the interview so that employers know you can be serious when you need to be. Tell stories of how you encouraged or motivated others in a way that had a positive impact.

How to succeed: You easily draw others to you with your infectious enthusiasm. Visualize the best possible outcome and orient your tasks and productivity toward that goal. Your natural optimism keeps you adaptable to possible roadblocks as you get started.

Sharpen your talent with these questions:

Where can you use your expertise to encourage others?

What knowledge or ideas do you have that you can get others excited about?

What examples can you think of where your positivity made an impact on a project or on your team?

What are you enthusiastic about that you can share with others?

Khristina B, USA

I have been in the medical field my entire career. I've had many roles throughout the last 30 years, but it wasn't until recently when I finally got an opportunity to put my Relator to task. I was working from home, without a team, in credentialing. It was a very detailed field with little people interaction. It was draining.

Then I began working as a recruiter staffing for nurses. It's a position that I never thought I would do in a million years, and I love it! It's mostly because of the relational piece. Speaking with each nurse to find out what their needs are and what is going on in their lives. My goal is to find a contract that meets those criteria then have them as a client for the foreseeable future.

Being relationship-focused is what will make me successful in my new career path. For me laying a strong foundation builds solid relationships, so they refer their friends. In the staffing world this is called building your pipeline.

Changing paths in mid-life can be scary but also rewarding. I'm still in the medical field but work is fun again. Sometimes you don't need a new career, you just need to use the strengths God already gave you in a new way.

Relator®

RELATOR® for Career Success

You thrive in opportunities which allow you to foster long-term relationships, have one-on-ones on a regular basis, and work closely with a tight knit team. You prioritize people over tasks.

According to Gallup®: People exceptionally talented in the Relator theme enjoy close relationships with others. They find deep satisfaction in working hard with friends to achieve a goal.

Celebrate:

- Your loyalty and trustworthiness
- Your values of honesty and authenticity
- Your close circle of friends
- How easily you build relationships

Evaluate:

- Am I isolating people?
- Do I appear closed off or aloof?
- Do I play favorites?
- Am I holding any grudges?

What to look for: Look for opportunities which allow you to establish close working relationships and foster loyalty among colleagues and/or stakeholders. You will appreciate positions which allow you time to develop a long-term connection that builds trust. Opportunities where interacting with people is core to the job will keep you motivated and engaged.

How to search: Find a peer you trust to help you in the search process. Your close circle will help you network by introducing you to the people who are most likely able to help you. Having a confidant through the process will keep you energized and focused and help you make the best decision. Take time to talk with people you know about their paths and ask for advice.

What to communicate: You can quickly build rapport during the interview by asking questions not only about the job or the company, but about the personal career path of the interviewer. Give examples of how you created loyal connections and created a solid level of trust in your past jobs. Tell stories of how you benefited past organizations through your relationship-building.

How to succeed: Consider finding a mentor early on to help you acclimate. Remember to make sure the relationships you are cultivating are the ones which will help you be most successful in your personal goals as well as those of the company. Get to know your close coworkers by participating in team building activities, partnering with others, and collaborating on projects.

Sharpen your talent with these questions:

What professional setting will allow you to join a team of people you would like to work closely with?

How can you leverage an existing relationship for a referral to a new career or company?

When have you created value for your previous employers by developing strong relationships with customers or clients?

How can you best prioritize getting to know the people on your team or the people you are serving?

'G' Gehan H-A, USA

Just prior to learning about CliftonStrengths® in 2013, I was released from a Financial Analyst-Specialist role I'd struggled in for two years. I'd tried to make it work despite it being a departure from my human resources skillset and wanting to "stick it out" for my team. I was miserable and knew it was a poor fit, but unaware of the underlying "why."

When I took Strengths, I learned "Analytical" was #30, with "Responsibility" then at #5 (WOO was #1) and themes and skills leaned toward more "generalist" wiring versus "specialist." Upon retake in 2021, "Responsibility" reflected as #1.

My realization/lesson learned years after my first test take is I've been more strategic in carefully selecting roles I'll more likely enjoy and showcase my talents, versus knowingly risk putting myself and others through anything similarly unfair to all involved.

Responsibility®

RESPONSIBILITY® for Career Success

You thrive in positions which have clear job duties and expectations are well defined. You appreciate that both outcome and process are celebrated and recognized.

According to Gallup®: People exceptionally talented in the Responsibility theme take psychological ownership of what they say they will do. They are committed to stable values such as honesty and loyalty.

Celebrate:

- Your word is your bond
- People trust you
- Honoring your commitments
- Your accountability

Evaluate:

- Am I micromanaging?
- Do I have clear boundaries?
- Am I over-committed?
- When do I say no?

What to look for: Look for organizations that value commitment and accountability. Search for roles which allow you to demonstrate your dedication and commitment to deliver, especially where others are counting on you for results. Clear deadlines and expectations are keys for your success. You also tend to enjoy volunteer opportunities so, consider organizations which have a service orientation.

How to search: Clearly outline each step to finding your dream position including where to network, employer follow-up, and thank you notes. You tend to be on task and focused when it comes to the job search. Using a well-defined process on how to find the job will help you focus and narrow your search. You can do this by working with someone, networking with others or even reading a how-to book.

What to communicate: Give examples of big projects that you completed successfully and use numbers to show the scope of what you were responsible for (team size, budget, etc). Tell stories about how you followed through to meet deadlines and share impressive metrics.

How to succeed: Be sure to set clear boundaries and expectations. You will be at your best when you are accountable to someone or something else as your desire to get things done is externally focused. Ask questions to understand the scope of a project before committing; remember, when you say yes to something you're saying no to something else.

Sharpen your talent with these questions:

How can you identify positions which will keep you from overextending yourself?

What areas of expertise are you uniquely equipped to be responsible for?

How can you highlight your ability to keep promises as you interview for new jobs?

Where can you volunteer to take on tasks that lighten the load of others while still able to balance your own tasks?

Leanna I, USA

As a Healthcare Recruiter for travel nurses, I am in a unique position where I not only prospect and find jobs for nurses, but I assist in ensuring their experience is successful so that they rebook with us after their 3-month contracts end. My Restorative strength shines through in my ability to never give up on them in the job search and work experience. I am constantly searching for the best solutions on how to better market them to facilities, how to ensure smoother communication with their team members. and how to prepare them for an ever-changing market.

That being said, my Restorative nature challenges me too; when I encounter problems that are outside of my power to fix (a job cancellation, pay changes, or internal communications), I have to constantly remind myself to stop fixating on the problem and focus on what is in my control. At the end of the day, my company and my nurses know I will fight relentlessly to ensure their success and happiness. While my Restorative strength has its ups and downs, it challenges me to grow both personally and professionally and I wouldn't trade that for the world.

Restorative™

RESTORATIVE™ for Career Success

You thrive in environments which allow you to solve challenging problems. You don't fear a challenge, but rather enjoy identifying issues and navigating complex and difficult situations.

According to Gallup®: People exceptionally talented in the Restorative theme are adept at dealing with problems. They are good at figuring out what is wrong and resolving it.

Celebrate:

- How you solve problems
- The ease with which you handle difficult decisions
- Your commitment to doing things right
- Being solution-oriented

Evaluate:

- Is my focus more negative than positive?
- Am I fixated on problems rather than solutions?
- Am I being overly critical (of myself or others)?
- Is my viewpoint too narrow?

What to look for: Search for roles where problem-solving and finding unique solutions is a big part of your responsibility. Start-ups and mergers could provide unique opportunities for you to dive in with your ability to see what needs to be fixed and go after it head-on. Roles that allow you to identify what's not working, along with the authority to implement solutions, will be a great fit in any size organization.

How to search: Make a list of the challenges you most prefer. Are they people focused? Process focused? Or product focused? Once you've narrowed this part down, begin to search for roles or companies which align with your interest. Identify whether a change in role, company, industry, culture, pay or location is the primary driver for your search to resolve whatever wasn't satisfying in your last job.

What to communicate: Consider making a pros and cons list of your own abilities before going into the interview. This will help you prepare your answers and highlight your strengths, while demonstrating how you also overcome challenges. Talk about past challenges you've faced and how you successfully found a solution. Sharing those positive results is key so they can easily see how you solved the problem.

How to succeed: A new job is just a new challenge for you and learning about the challenges in the new environment fills you with energy as you know where you can have the biggest impact. Remember to focus on your own tasks and projects, rather than focusing on issues that are not in your area of responsibility.

Sharpen your talent with these questions:

What problems or challenges exist in the world that you'd like to help solve?

How can you research where your background best contributes to finding solutions?

What problems have you solved in the past that are relevant to the ones presented in this new role?

How can you identify challenges in your new organization and volunteer to help bring solutions?

Elisa L, Mexico

Self-Assurance has helped me since I was in college and made a last-minute decision to take an internship in Spain. I arrived there alone, with no friends, without basic information, the address of the University or even some place to live; but I did have the solid intention to have a job to earn enough money to travel around Europe by myself. At the end of the year, I achieved everything I had intended to achieve.

Professionally, I had the courage to leave a prosperous job at an incredible international company to become an entrepreneur and open my own business. I currently own a carwash with 20 employees. Additionally, I founded OD Consulting. I know I wouldn't have achieved all of this without trusting myself.

Self-Assurance has even saved my life, some years ago I almost drowned at the sea, my self-confidence empowered me to swim to shore and avoid being pulled by the tide. I always had the certainty that I would be ok.

Self-Assurance®

SELF-ASSURANCE® for Career Success

> *You thrive in environments which allow you to have a certain amount of autonomy in your decision making, where you are surrounded by a competent team and there is a clear path for leadership roles.*

According to Gallup®: People exceptionally talented in the Self-Assurance theme feel confident in their ability to take risks and manage their own lives. They have an inner compass that gives them certainty in their decisions.

Celebrate:

- Your internal confidence
- Your ability to provide reassurance when others are in doubt
- Your steadiness in rocky situations
- The confidence you instill in others

Evaluate:

- Am I being dismissive of the opinions of others?
- Am I being stubborn?
- Am I being too authoritative?
- Am I impatient with others' insecurities?

What to look for: Search for positions that provide natural opportunities for leadership or fast growth into leadership roles. You appreciate organizations that aren't afraid of taking risks occasionally as you like to test the boundaries of your own abilities and break away from the status quo.

How to search: Even if you feel quite confident in the job search, it can always be of value to gain perspective from others you trust. Solicit recommendations from those you've worked with who can help highlight your strengths and abilities. Share what you're looking for with your network and the value you bring so they can help you find the right opportunities. Think about the types of challenges you most enjoy and seek roles that will allow you to take the helm quickly.

What to communicate: Demonstrate your risk tolerance by talking about past projects where taking a calculated risk paid off. Your confidence in yourself and your abilities will be obvious but remember to keep it balanced and show that you are willing to learn on the job as well. Ask about who supports you in your role as the competence of others is especially important to you.

How to succeed: You easily adapt to the new job as you are confident that you can tackle the tasks and challenges that come your way. Remember that being vulnerable on occasion can help you build stronger relationships with your co-workers.

Sharpen your talent with these questions:

Where do you have the most confidence that you can make a difference?

In what setting or with what subject do you have the most expertise to leverage in your next role?

How has having the confidence to take risks in the past turned out with great results?

How can you gain confidence in your new role and also spend time learning about your new coworkers' areas of expertise?

Jennifer M, USA

Significance in service of others is the guiding rudder in my work. As I reflect on my three careers, I see how it consistently guided my decisions and actions. The common theme is the ability to make a difference in the lives of others. As a political team member, I helped candidates I believed in get elected. While in public service, I drove strategy helping others find employment in quality jobs. For the past 15 yrs I've served as a leader in nonprofit, mission-driven associations. In each role when I experienced success, I felt the impact deeply and it motivated me forward. Often, this drive and commitment was viewed by others as trying to "outshine" someone else. I even recall being asked by my boss after a keynote speech, "What are you doing on stage? Everyone keeps talking about it." It was a pivotal moment in our relationship. I was sharing stories and motivating action for others to lead. It sounds simple when I look back, I was compelled to motivate others to lead. My boss however, viewed it as taking over. My boss left the organization shortly after and rumors swirled that I "pushed her out." It's important to understand your power and edge. It is not just about the often-misunderstood drive for recognition. Frequently, it can be a drive for purpose and impact. It took me almost 30 years to understand and appreciate that.

Significance®

SIGNIFICANCE® for Career Success

> *You thrive in organizations where making a big impression and having a lasting impact are part of the core vision and purpose. You easily step into the spotlight.*

According to Gallup®: People exceptionally talented in the Significance theme want to make a big impact. They are independent and prioritize projects based on how much influence they will have on their organization or people around them.

Celebrate:

- Your free and independent spirit
- Your desire to make a positive difference
- Your drive to succeed
- Your comfort in the spotlight

Evaluate:

- Am I seeking recognition for the right things?
- Do I have a healthy balance between emotional and material success?
- Do I push others into the spotlight even if they are uncomfortable?
- Does my network serve a purpose or am I just "rubbing elbows"?

What to look for: Search for organizations which will recognize your efforts and where you can have a lasting impact on the company or the lives of others. You appreciate companies which have a rewards program or strong recognition culture in place. You might also consider roles where you can be "the face" of the company.

How to search: Consider making a list of areas where you feel you could have a big impact or make a difference. What causes are you passionate about? With whom do you want to leave a lasting impression? Is being in the spotlight important to you? Answer these questions to narrow down your options and focus on roles which will satisfy those needs.

What to communicate: Demonstrate your motivation to have a lasting impact in your role. Share past experiences where you have held a role in the public eye or had a profound influence on those around you. Express your desire to continue growing and serving in this new role. Remember to ask questions of the interviewer as well to show your interest in learning more about them and/or the company.

How to succeed: You will easily set yourself apart from the crowd as you quickly take on challenging and meaningful tasks. Recognize where your co-workers are shining and praise them as well. While they may not enjoy the spotlight like you do, they will appreciate being valued.

Sharpen your talent with these questions:

What would you like to be known for and in what setting could your contributions be noticed?

Who could write you a recommendation and in what format would that be most valuable to you?

Are there professional associations that might appreciate your involvement and give you a bigger platform?

How can you volunteer for a visible project with noticeable impact?

Joseph W, USA

In the mortgage world, Strategic allows me to see further than my counterparts and colleagues. I provide direction and vision, while also anticipating obstacles, and preparing solutions to problems that others may not even know exist. It's incredibly validating when someone says: "That thing you said would happen... well it happened. Now, can you help me?"

I've discovered that finding the right team is of utmost importance. My attention is most often focused on the horizon. Influencers help make the abstract or invisible into something concrete and actionable. Relationship Builders keep everyone together through the instability of vision-initiated change. Executors ensure the paths laid out in moments of clarity are followed diligently.

Strategic enables me to see a variety of routes to a given destination. Rather than being limited to one rigid path, this affords me tremendous flexibility, both during the planning phase and during the implementation phase when unforeseen obstacles get in the way.

This gives me tremendous confidence in leadership within my professional context. When a team member is struggling in a particular role, or an initiative is not panning out according to the plan, I find it easy to adjust on the fly. Usually, I will have already considered the possibility that "Plan A" was not going to work, so initiating "Plan B" is no big deal.

Strategic®

STRATEGIC® for Career Success

> *You thrive in roles where creativity and flexibility are part of your everyday responsibilities and there's more than one way to reach a goal. You love exploring multiple paths to a destination.*

According to Gallup®: People exceptionally talented in the Strategic theme create alternative ways to proceed. Faced with any given scenario, they can quickly spot the relevant patterns and issues.

Celebrate:

- How plan B is just the beginning for you
- You see patterns that others don't
- Your seemingly intuitive nature
- Your ability to see the "big picture"

Evaluate:

- Have I thought this through?
- Am I making the best choice?
- Am I considering others' opinions?
- Am I communicating my idea clearly?

What to look for: Roles where you can consult on desired outcomes could be a great fit. Also consider organizational roles that require exploring solutions to current challenges, allow for creativity and out-of-the-box thinking as well as some flexibility in how things are done.

How to search: Start with the goal in mind. Knowing what you want will help you create the path to get there. Contact your network to learn about different options which might yield a similar result - be it role, company or industry. They might see something you haven't considered. A pros and cons list will help you narrow down your options when the offers come.

What to communicate: Highlight your ability to see the "big picture" and then create the path to accomplish the goal. Think through different scenarios before the interview to help prepare your answers ahead of time, allowing you to respond more naturally in the moment. Tell stories of how you tried different tactics to accomplish something that maybe wasn't necessarily the first idea but yielded good results.

How to succeed: Take in the overall workings of your area and the company to prioritize how you network, with whom you can collaborate best, and channels you may need to explore further. You might need to clarify your plans as others might not see the solution as easily as you do. Let those you work with know that you see different possible paths to a target and that you value the ideas they bring as well.

Sharpen your talent with these questions:

How can you identify what you need from a job in order to realize there might be several different possibilities that would accomplish that?

What are the values driving your job search and what are all the possible ways to accomplish them?

What have you accomplished in the past that benefitted from your out of the box thinking?

How can you learn about the strategic plan of your organization and understand what has already been tried or planned so that you can bring additional ideas?

Tobias W, USA

I use my WOO (Winning Others Over) naturally by seeking the thrill of meeting new people and making connections to expand my network. I work in Emergency Management preparing for disasters. I used to see WOO as persuasion, but I found it was more about how I won over the respect and admiration of others because of how I interact with them rather than trying to convince them to approve of me or my ideas. I made it my goal at work to find out what people needed in their roles to be successful or better prepared and worked to meet their needs while aligning it with my job. I frequently visited staff during all shifts to discuss issues relating to their roles and either discussing options or coaching them in response and preparedness topics. I found ways to practice and train with them so it didn't over burden their busy schedules but focused on efforts to practice skills and increase staff capabilities. I also enjoy meaningful discussions to draw people into conversations both in-person and online. Authentic conversation is the best way to connect with others as well as the best way for me to learn. It is because of this easy nature to converse and help others that I can Win Others Over.

WOO®

WOO® for Career Success

You thrive in roles where networking and speaking with others is a key part of your position as people naturally gravitate to you. You prefer social interaction over solitary roles.

According to Gallup®: People exceptionally talented in the WOO theme love the challenge of meeting new people and winning them over. They derive satisfaction from breaking the ice and making a connection with someone.

Celebrate:

- Your ability to make everyone feel at home
- Your outgoing nature
- How you start conversations with ease
- You make socializing look easy

Evaluate:

- Am I coming off as shallow?
- Am I showing genuine interest in those I'm connecting with?
- Am I overshadowing others around me?
- Is my energy matching the room?

What to look for: Look for opportunities where you can make connections with other people both internally and externally. Forming relationships is rewarding for you, so positions which require you to network, sell, or do publicity could attract you. A natural fit includes roles that involve influencing people or outcomes.

How to search: Your social network is the best place for you to start. You know a wide variety of people and connecting with them will energize you in your search. Ask for introductions to help you advance your search and open new doors for you. Be bold and reach out to people in the field or company that interests you and suggest a networking meeting. Cold calling is a fun challenge and could yield a beneficial connection.

What to communicate: Share experiences where you have successfully engaged with a network of people and quickly established rapport. Demonstrate how your connections have helped you create solutions and meet goals. Your high energy can be contagious, just be sure to not be too overly enthusiastic by gauging the energy level of your interviewer.

How to succeed: You easily connect with your co-workers and make them feel comfortable around you and this creates a team atmosphere. Remember to maintain a certain level of professionalism and not become too familiar too quickly. Keep it fun and keep it professional. Volunteer for roles where you are in front of new contacts or welcoming new or potential clients.

Sharpen your talent with these questions:

In which kind of environments or situations do you feel most comfortable making new connections?

Who would you like to connect with to learn more about the field you're interested in?

When and where have you been successful at WOOing?

Make a list. Who do you need to know and how can you make the connection?

Final Thoughts

I hope you have found the information included in this book useful to you. Whether you are on the search for a new career, trying to make the most of the one you're in or simply helping others find their calling, it is our wish that your talents are maximized and your potential is realized.

Heck, it's my mission: *To live in a world where talents aren't wasted, potentials are realized, and happiness is contagious.* It's the backbone to everything I do, including - and most especially - this series of books.

If you are interested in deepening your knowledge through a strengths lens, please check out the page http://discoverjoself.com/practical-strengths-programs There you will find opportunities to deep dive into your own talents and grow with a group of peer mentors who are looking to do the same.

Other books in the Practical Strengths series:

- Parenting (can be purchased on Amazon)
  https://www.amazon.com/Practical-Strengths-Parenting-CliftonStrengths-Everyday/dp/B08XLGGFY8/

Coming Soon…

- Communication
- Relationships
- Habits & Goal Setting
- Spirituality & Philosophy
- Health and Fitness.
- Recreation & Hobbies

If you'd like to be informed of new releases and occasional updates, as well as download strengths-specific memes, additional workbooks, and have the opportunity to be a part of the future books by sharing your own story, please visit: http://discoverjoself.com/resources

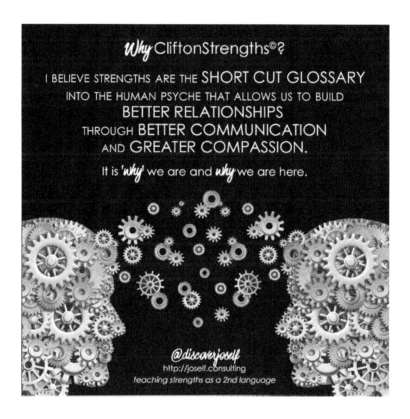

About the Author

Jo Self is on a mission to teach CliftonStrengths® as a second Language. She seeks to create a world where everyone can live to their full potential, talents aren't wasted, and happiness is contagious. As a single mompreneur and expat - spending 11 years in Peru and recently relocated to Mexico - she understands the challenges and rewards that both entail. When she's not helping others create extraordinary lives, she can be found at the sewing machine, at the movies, enjoying a glass of wine with friends or horsing around with her terribly precocious little boy, affectionately known as O.

In the past, Jo developed nationally recognized and award-winning employee programs for Yum! Brands, the world's largest fast food restaurant company. And when she wasn't leading in-house teams to discover their strengths, she was on loan to other organizations helping them to do the same – all while serving on the national board of directors for her professional organization, ESM Association.

Once she left the corporate ranks, she started her own event business, Bon Vivant Savant, and was recognized as both a "Top Female Under 40" influencer in the community by Louisville Woman Magazine and also as a leading entrepreneur in the "40 under 40" list by Business Week Magazine.

After leaving the States and moving to Peru in 2011, her entrepreneurial spirit continued with a tourism start-up that won a government grant as well as being recognized by ADEX as a top 50 start-up in the country. However, with all of these achievements, she still wasn't feeling fulfilled. A health scare in early 2015 set her on a course of self-reflection which brought her back to what she had always done best, had made her happy *and* given her joy. That answer was Strengths. She immediately contacted Gallup® and began the journey for what she now confirms is her true calling, being a Gallup®® Certified Strengths Coach.

Embracing her own strengths-based life led to the creation of her course, The Language of You. She guides other coaches and heart-based entrepreneurs to align their mission with their message, connecting them to their ideal clients. She also works with larger organizations to improve communication, leading to higher engagement and better relationships among team members.

"It is my deep desire to share with the world the power and gift that the CliftonStrengths® language provides. It is the heart of this book series, Practical Strengths. I believe that sharing this language with one another leads to improving relationships through better communication and greater compassion for one another."

CONNECT WITH JO:

https://www.linkedin.com/in/joself/ http://discoverjoself.com

References

If you'd like to explore further:

Assessments

CliftonStrengths® for Students for ages 15-21
https://www.strengthsquest.com/

CliftonStrengths®
https://www.Gallup®.com/cliftonstrengths/

(I do not make any profit from sharing these links above)

Related books:

StrengthsFinder 2.0 by Tom Rath

CliftonStrengths® for Students by Gallup®®

Strengths-Based Leadership by Gallup®®

Please visit http://discoverjoself.com/resources for more information on books and assessments along with my guidance for how to get the most out of the materials.

Printed in Great Britain
by Amazon

41381573R00096